CEO

WHO GETS TO THE TOP

IN

AMERICA

CEO

WHO GETS TO THE TOP
—————— IN ——————
AMERICA

by

David L. Kurtz
Louis E. Boone
C. Patrick Fleenor

89-1154

Michigan State University Press
East Lansing, Michigan
1989

Michigan State University Press
East Lansing, Michigan 48823-5202

Production: Julie L. Loehr
Editing: Anne Forgrave
Cover Design: Lynne A. Brown
Typography: the Copyfitters, Ltd.
Printing: Edward Brothers, Inc.

Library of Congress Cataloging-in-Publication Data

Kurtz, David L.
    CEO: who gets to the top in America.

    1. Chief executive officers–United States.
I. Boone, Louis, E.   II. Fleenor, C. Patrick,
1938-   .   III. Title.
HD38.25.U6K87   1989   658.4   88-42902
ISBN 0-87013-261-X

to
Diane,
Pat, and
Margaret

CONTENTS

LIST OF TABLES

"Eagles don't flock—
you have to find them one at a time."

H. Ross Perot

PREFACE

CEO: Who Gets to the Top in America? is the result of a comprehensive study of chief executive officers of America's corporate giants. Instead of relying on a few selected interviews, the book is developed from personal information provided by over 200 CEOs. Chief executives in every business sector are represented, including J. Peter Grace of W. R. Grace, Paul Oreffice of Dow Chemical, David M. Roderick of USX Corporation, Peter A. Magowan of Safeway Stores, Inc., Arthur O. Sulzberger of *The New York Times*, and T. Boone Pickens, Jr. of Mesa Petroleum.

The data provide a comprehensive, revealing profile of the nation's chief executive officers. The cooperation of these corporate titans in providing personal information produced a multidimensional portrait of their childhoods, the influence of their parents, the role of education in their successes, and dozens of other factors as diverse as leisure time pursuits, birth order, physical characteristics, marriage, work experiences in high school and college, religion, smoking and drinking habits, and personal management styles. The result is a definitive portrait of who gets to the top of corporate America, and a set of standards against which aspiring chief executive officers can measure their own attributes and assess the likelihood of ever residing in the corner office on the top floor.

A project of this magnitude would never have been completed without the assistance of many people. The authors are deeply indebted to the 243 CEOs whose names are listed in the Appendix. These executives who took time out of their busy schedules to answer our dozens of questions made this book possible.

We would also like to thank our research associates, Judy Block, Colleen Keleher, Nancy Moudry, and Ken Thomas for their numerous contributions to the book. Finally, appreciation must be expressed for our capable secretarial corps, including Ruby Gardner, Jeanne Lowe, and Linda Troup.

"That's the American way. If little kids don't aspire to make money like I did, what the hell good is this country?"

Lee Iacocca[1]

PROLOGUE

A new aristocracy has developed in the United States. This new elite is made up of the heads of America's largest corporations: the chief executive officers, or CEOs. Let's take a historical look at how this happened.

How Today's Corporate Aristocracy Developed

The general public's attitude toward business—and the people at a corporation's helm—has been complex and frequently contradictory. But such almost schizophrenic feelings are understandable when one considers that business is both employer and servant, producer and polluter, benefactor and aggressor.

The two images of Henry Ford that emerged over the first half of the twentieth century illustrate this contradiction. Ford, obsessed with his dream of converting the motor car from a plaything of the rich to a replacement for the horse of the public, had the stuff of which folk heroes are made. When Ford built his first horseless carriage in 1893, the price tag was $9,000. Every piece of the automobile was hand-designed, and the emphasis was on high prices for limited production runs.

Ford saw a different strategy. If the horseless carriage could be mass-produced, a firm could earn small profits on each car sold and reduce the price to fit the budget of most families. Ford found a solution in using vanadium steel for automobile bodies and inventing a fast-moving assembly line. Worker morale was boosted tremendously through the adoption of a shorter, eight-hour workday. Ford shocked U.S. industry by paying his employees $5 a day, more than double the prevailing wages in similar industries. And his strategy worked. By 1908, his Model T carried a price tag of $850. In 1926, the price had dropped to $284. By that time, nearly 15 million Model Ts had been sold.

From this success, the production genius acquired an image of an ordinary man made extraordinary by hard work and perseverance, an eccentric idealist who cared enough about the world's people to sail for Europe in 1915 in his "peace ship" in a quixotic effort to end the war.

But there was a second Ford: an ignorant, practically illiterate man who seldom read books because "they mess up my mind." The second Ford was a steadfast anti-Semite, as well as a bigot in general. In the factory, his refusal to add technological improvements to the Model T such as hydraulic brakes and a six-cylinder engine paved the way for General Motors and Chrysler to make major inroads on Ford's share of the automobile market. Ford ignored important marketing considerations ("they [consumers] can have any color they want, as long as it is black!"), and his competitors capitalized on these deficiencies. His militant opposition to unionization left scars on Ford union-management relations for years. His unwillingness to permit any semblance of organization within Ford Motor Company in spite of his advancing age and growing senility almost ruined the firm.

Ford, like Cornelius Vanderbilt, Andrew Carnegie, Cyrus McCormick, and John D. Rockefeller, was a man of unusual ability whose talents and opportunities coincided at the right moment in history. Both Ford and Carnegie were deeply influenced by their strict upbringings and by deeply religious, evangelical mothers. Both purchased a bit of immortality through giving away much of what they had earned during their lifetimes. Carnegie's 1889 article, *The Disgrace of Dying Rich*, advocated charitable uses of wealth. By the time of his death in 1919, the founder of the company that was to become U.S. Steel had distributed over

$350 million to foundations and causes ranging from libraries, museums, and universities to pensions for all Civil War telegraphers.

John D. Rockefeller, too, turned charitable benefactor late in life, but he also possessed a negative image as one of the nation's "robber barons" because of fierce, unrelenting efforts to drive out competitors. His decision in 1892 to slash the price of Standard Oil kerosene in Denver to $7^{1}/_{2}$ cents per gallon to eliminate competition there, while maintaining the 25 cents per gallon price elsewhere, produced ill will among heating oil customers throughout the nation. Such actions only fueled the belief among the general public that all business titans subscribed to the attitude expressed by the son of Cornelius Vanderbilt: "The public be damned!"

This negative image began to appear in literature, in films, and in such antitrust legislation as the Sherman Antitrust Act and the Clayton Act. Upton Sinclair's *The Jungle* exposed the horrors of the meat packing industry. The classic film *Citizen Kane* based its chief character on the wealthy and influential newspaper titan William Randolph Hearst. As the business historian C. Northcote Parkinson expressed it:

> Rarely has the business man been depicted as a hero by those most influential in forming public opinion. In literature, the values of commerce have often been contrasted with the values of gentility and charity; among social historians the evils of factory masters and the amorality of the industrial manipulators have received more emphasis than the romance of enterprise; and among economists the terms "monopoly" and "oligopoly" imply a criticism which suggests more than just "healthy competition." Indeed, the word "enterprise" suggests initiative, daring, and imagination. Put the adjectives "large," "corporate" in front and very different connotations appear: something unwieldy, parasitic and predatory comes to mind.[2]

In many instances, much of the negative images of individual corporations faded following the deaths of their founders. Family dynasties formed in a few instances, such as the Ford, the Rockefeller, and the Philips in Europe. The son of

Cornelius Vanderbilt proved even more adept at making money than did his father. By the time he died in 1877, the railway and shipping baron Cornelius Vanderbilt was generally considered to be the founder of big business in modern times as well as the richest man in the United States. Vanderbilt's son succeeded in doubling his $105 million inheritance to become the richest man in the world.

But successes of children and grandchildren such as Henry Ford II were largely exceptions. In general, the successors of Getty, Carnegie, and Chrysler were salaried professional managers. And the more recent candidates for inclusion as founders of major corporations—Edwin Land, An Wang, David Packard—are more likely to be, in the words of one observer, "white-coated technocrats, men of mystery, priests of the computer, and experts in accountancy. There is little place, it would seem, in advanced technology for robber barons and ruthless warfare."[3] With a few notable exceptions, such as the eccentric film magnate, aircraft manufacturer, hotel owner, and full-time oddity Howard Hughes, these second, third, and fourth generation CEOs proved to be a group of colorless executives who kept a low profile. Although they were well rewarded, they (and their compensations) were largely unknown to the American public. But over the past 25 years, business in general has been forced to adopt a more public stand on a variety of issues. As a result, the CEO has been thrust into the limelight.

The case of Lee Iacocca is illustrative of this trend. While Iacocca was well known in business circles, he was virtually unknown to the general public. His firing by Henry Ford II received some notoriety, but except in Detroit the story was relegated to the business page of newspapers across the United States. Iacocca became a public figure when he appealed to the federal government for a financial bailout to save Chrysler Corporation. His public image was, of course, enhanced further through Chrysler's advertising featuring this tough-talking CEO. Next came Iacocca's best-selling autobiography, and today there is even talk of the White House.

Along with the CEOs' higher profiles came bigger and bigger compensation packages. In fact, these sizable rewards actively contributed to the CEOs' higher profiles. Publications such as *Forbes, Fortune, The Wall Street Journal, Business Week*, and *U.S. News & World Report* all carried stories analyzing CEO compensation. In effect, these reports have made executive pay a public issue.

Few can argue about the noteworthiness of CEO compensation, for many of the numbers are mindboggling. In 1986, Iacocca's efforts resulted in total pay—including salary, bonuses, and long-term compensation—of $20.5 million. He was joined in the eight-figure compensation elite by Reebok International chairman Paul Fireman, who garnered total pay of $13 million in 1986. This amounts to slightly less than $35,000 a day for all 365 days.

If we drop to the seven-figure category, we find that chief executives of 30 of the 100 largest industrial companies earned $1 million or more last year. In fact, the median cash compensation for the top 100 CEOs last year was $923,110.[4]

But is money the primary motivation that propels these executives to the top? Are they likely to agree with another individual who only a few years ago was acclaimed as the world's best at his chosen vocation? The man is former Heavyweight Boxing Champion Larry Holmes. He has summed up his motivation this way: "Why do you think I'm fighting? The glory? The agony of defeat? You show me a man says he ain't fighting for money, I'll show you a fool."[5]

Clearly, money and the trappings of wealth are important considerations in the career choices of these executives; but seldom, if ever, is money a primary source of motivation. Virtually all of today's big business leaders would subscribe to John D. Rockefeller's belief about personal wealth as a motivator. The Standard Oil founder put it this way: "Mere money-making has never been my goal." In fact, Atari founder Nolan Bushnell accurately described the role of executive compensation as a motivator in a recent interview. He said, "Business is a good game—lots of competition and a minimum of rules. You keep score with money."[6]

If Not Money, Then What?

Huge compensation packages have made America's CEOs a new corporate aristocracy. This image is further solidified by their expanded public image. But what made them what they are and how did they get where they are today?

The authors began their study of CEOs over six years ago. The data base is limited, consisting primarily of anecdotal case studies in the form of articles and biographies. In addition, magazines such as *Forbes* have published annual surveys, and the executive search firm Heidrick & Struggles periodically develops a profile of American CEOs. But no truly comprehensive, three-dimensional report exists that delves into the family background, social class, personal characteristics, personal habits, religion, education, early years, leisure activities, and managerial style of a CEO that combine to make him unique; thus, this study was born.

Methodology

An extensive questionnaire focusing on all of these topics was forwarded to CEOs of the 800 largest industrial and service organizations in the United States. The 243 corporate leaders who provided the source materials for *CEO: Who Gets to the Top in America?* are listed in the Appendix. The authors hope that others who aspire to corporate leadership will be helped by the information they provided.

A Word About Women

One readily identifiable characteristic of America's corporate leaders is that they are almost exclusively men. In searching through directories of CEOs of the largest industrial corporations and service organizations, only four exceptions to the male-dominated corporate hierarchy occur: Katharine Graham of the Washington Post Company, Elisabeth Ortenberg of Liz Claiborne, Karen Horn of Bank One-Cleveland, and Marion O. Sandler, who shares the position of CEO at Golden West Financial with her husband.

However, there is increasing evidence that the next generation of the nation's CEOs will not remain a fraternity. Women comprise almost half of all university students majoring in business. A recent *Business Week* compilation of 50 fast-track young managers included 14 women executives. Women included on this roster of some of the most successful young managers in America are the vice president of finance and administration at American Airlines, Apple Computer's vice president for manufacturing, one of Xerox Corporation's youngest plant managers, Scott Paper's corporate planning manager, and the senior vice president for administration at Navistar International.[7] Talented female executives such as these increase the likelihood that more of tomorrow's CEOs will be women.

1. "Overheard," *Newsweek,* 11 May 1987, 15; "Now Hear This," *Fortune,* 25 May 1987, 14.
2. C. Northcote Parkinson, *Big Business* (Boston: Little, Brown, 1974), 16.
3. Parkinson, 128.
4. "Million-Dollar Club Grows," *The Wall Street Journal,* 11 November 1986, 1.
5. "Now Hear This," *Fortune,* 10 December 1984, 11.
6. Robert Byrne, *The Third, and Possibly the Best, 637 Best Things Anybody Ever Said* (New York: Atheneum, 1986), 202.
7. "Is There a Future CEO in this Bunch?" *Business Week,* 10 November 1986, 97.

"My father was a pretty sharp businessman, and he said he thought GM was the best-managed company in the world. He suggested I give them a try, so I did."

Roger Smith
CEO, General Motors
Corporation[1]

1

FAMILY BACKGROUND

The path to the CEO's four P's—pay, power, perks, and prestige—begins in infancy. Everything from relationships with parents to family size and birth order affects a person's life in general and, as a consequence, his business career. Mesa Petroleum CEO T. Boone Pickens, Jr. credits his father with directing him to a future in oil: "It was my father who forced me into geology in college when, at 17, I didn't know what to do."[2] In the case of GM's Roger Smith, his father talked him out of plans to join the rapidly growing aerospace industry, and he went to work for the auto giant instead.

THE INFLUENCE OF PARENTS

In both direct and indirect ways, many fathers and mothers have charted the business careers of their off-spring.[3] Some CEOs, such as August A. Busch III of Anheuser-Busch, J. Peter Grace of W. R. Grace, and Arthur O. Sulzberger of *The New York Times*, were formally groomed to take over the positions held by their fathers. Many others had fathers who were less direct in guiding them toward a business career. William O'Neil, who founded General Tire and Rubber (now GenCorp), told his sons numerous stories about his work, and encouraged them to follow him into the business. The father of K Mart chairman Bernard Fauber practiced what he preached about hard work, followed Ben Franklin's classic "early to bed, early to rise" maxim, and extolled the value of getting a job done as soon as possible.

Mothers, too, have had a profound impact on the lives and careers of many CEOs. John F. Welch, Jr., the chief executive officer of General Electric, credits much of his self-confidence and drive to his mother. Welch, who has always been a stammerer, recalls, "She told me I didn't have a speech impediment . . . just that my brain worked too fast."[4] Welch's mother later supported him when he decided to abandon his family's blue-collar background by quitting a factory job that bored him.

Jerry Tsai of Commercial Credit Group Inc., relies on business advice from his mother, admitting that, "I can't remember a major deal I've done without sounding her out first."[5] Retailing giant Leslie Wexner, chairman of The Limited, Inc., runs his business with the energetic leadership inspired and exemplified by his mother as he was growing up: set high standards, work hard to reach them, and anything is possible. Today she is secretary of The Limited and her office at corporate headquarters is next to her son's.

Maybe J. W. McLean of the Banks of Mid-America summed it up best when he said, "The parental effect in my case was significant in terms of my father's solid commitment to his business . . . and my mother's perseverance and always positive attitude."

THE CEO's BIRTHPLACE

Some chief executive officers, such as C. R. Palmer of the Rowan Companies, believe that where they were reared had an impact on their future business careers. The West Texas native, whose values and ambitions were shaped by his schoolteacher parents and their struggles to survive the Great Depression, couldn't disagree more with the song title, "Happiness is Seeing Lubbock, Texas, in the Rearview Mirror."

Where are chief executives born and reared? Not unexpectedly, they come from all over, but certain patterns emerge. Most obvious is the prominence of New York, the birthplace of 109 of the 798 CEOs on a recent listing in *Forbes*. The next-largest providers of chief executives are the states of Illinois, claiming 50 CEOs; Pennsylvania (49); Texas (48); and Ohio (44). Following these states, in the 25–43 group, are New Jersey, Massachusetts, Missouri, and California.

It should be noted that a shift may be occurring in regard to birthplace. A survey of senior executives (not limited to CEOs) by Korn-Ferry International and the UCLA Graduate School of Management concluded that today's typical top executive grew up in the Midwest.

Some CEOs Are Foreign Born

Not all top officers of U.S. firms are Americans by birth. Heinz CEO Anthony J. F. O'Reilly was born and grew up in Ireland, and Jerry Tsai of American Can was born in Shanghai. Thirty-five of our CEOs, in fact, were born abroad, with Canada contributing the largest number (10), followed by England (4), Germany (3), Italy (3), France (2), Japan (2), and Poland (2). One each came from Austria, China, Ireland, Israel, the Netherlands, Palestine, Scotland, the Soviet Union, and Turkey.

What difference does birthplace make? To take an extreme example, consider the case of Robert Boizuetta, the Cuban-born chairman of The Coca-Cola Company. In 1985, the company replaced its 100-year-old formula for Coke with a new flavor. Despite assurances from its testing people that consumers preferred the new taste in blind comparisons, a huge public outcry resulted, and The Coca-Cola Company was forced to bring back the original formula. Several analysts argued that a contributing factor to the debacle was that many of the firm's top officers were foreign-born, and they underestimated the importance of Coke to the psyche of the American public. While there is no way to prove this, of course, the analysts raise an interesting possibility.

PRESENCE OF PARENTS

Almost 90 percent of the CEOs in our study came from the traditional two-parent household, while only 10 percent grew up in a one-parent household, and one in 100 lived with either one or two parents on a part-time basis. One CEO, Tom Monaghan of Domino's Pizza, was reared in a Catholic orphanage.

Since the time many of these CEOs were growing up, the American family has undergone changes. The most dramatic of these changes involve the burgeoning numbers of one-parent households and the number of married women working outside the home. The Ozzie and Harriet conception of a family, composed of a working father and a mother who stays home to take care of the children, describes less than one in three of today's families. In 1950, about 25 percent of all married women held jobs outside the home; today, over 50 percent do. In fact, almost half of mothers with children under a year old work. One U.S. family in six is currently headed by a single, divorced, or widowed woman.[6]

Studies have shown that the absence of a parent has a serious negative impact on a child's intellectual development. For instance, Sutton-Smith, et al., (1968) compared median scores on the American College Entrance Examination. They found that boys whose fathers were present in the family had a median score 18 points higher on the quantitative test and 6 points higher on the verbal test than those with fathers absent. For girls, an 11-point difference on the quantitative test existed, but there was little or no difference in the scores on language skills. Another interesting finding of this study is that children with a sibling of the same sex did not suffer as much from the father's absence as those who had a sibling of the opposite sex. The Sutton-Smith study also reported that the worst effects from a father's absence occurred for children between the ages of 5 and 10, with less severe effects when the absence occurred when the children were either under 5 or over 10.

FAMILY SIZE

A growing body of research suggests that the smaller a family is, the more intelligent the children will be. For example, University of Michigan psychologist Robert Zajonc points out that trends in Scholastic Aptitude Test (SAT) scores have closely followed the patterns of family size in America. His research indicates that children from smaller families go further in school and make higher scores on standardized intelligence tests, even when studies control for family income. What is unclear, however, is the cause of this relationship.

One possibility is that parents with fewer children have more time to spend with each of them. This seems to be especially significant in the case of only children—those "lonely onlies" who are consistently overrepresented among college students and among high achievers in all walks of life. Another explanation, advanced by James Higgins of Michigan State University, is that parents with lower IQs tend to have larger families. This would mean that the relationship is not really one of family size to intelligence, but more a reflection of the parents' intelligence.

Size of Families in Which the CEOs Grew Up

Before reviewing the size of the households in which today's CEOs were born and reared, some comparison data are needed. Of contemporary families with children, 42 percent have one child, 37 percent have two children, 15 percent have three, 4 percent have four, and only 2 percent have five or more offspring. This translates to a current median household size of 1.84 children.

But declining household size is a well-known characteristic of the past two decades. What about family size statistics for the time periods during which today's CEOs were born? In 1920, the typical family contained 4.3 children. By 1930, this number had declined to 2.1 children.

These statistics contrast greatly with the size of the households in which today's CEOs were born. Today's chief executive officers came from families with an average of 2.9 children. In fact, almost one-fourth of them grew up in households with four or more children, four times the number of today's households with family sizes that large. Particularly striking is the small number of one-child households in which today's CEOs grew up. Only 12 percent of today's CEOs were reared as lonely onlies.

Parents' Family Income and Family Size

After comparing the size of families in relationship to social class, we found that none of the CEOs with very rich or very poor backgrounds had been only children. In fact, it was only among respondents from an upper-lower or "working class" background that we found a substantial proportion of only children: almost 25 percent. Only children comprised approximately 10 percent of both upper-middle and lower-middle class respondents. Another noteworthy finding was that those CEOs who came from very poor, lower-lower class backgrounds did, in fact, come from very large families. Fully 50 percent of these executives came from families with six or more children.

Table 1–1 shows the relationship between social class and number of children in the families in which the CEOs grew up. This chart should be read across; that is, each class listed on the bottom was broken down into the percentage with number of children as shown in the columns.

As can be seen, the smallest family sizes were in the two middle and the upper-lower class categories. These three groups were very close in size, with an average of about 2.6 children for the upper-lower class, 2.7 for the

Table 1–1: Social Class and Number of Children

		Percentage With			
Social Class	1 Child	2 Children	3 Children	4 Children	5 or more Children
Upper-upper	0	33	11	33	22
Lower-upper	0	25	38	13	25
Upper-middle	12	38	28	10	13
Lower-middle	11	34	34	16	5
Upper-lower	24	27	30	6	12
Lower-lower	0	0	25	25	50

lower-middle class, and 2.8 for the upper-middle class families. Lower-lower class families were, as stated, the largest, averaging about 5.25 children, while upper-upper class families had approximately 3.6 children, and lower-upper class families had about 3.75 children.

BIRTH ORDER

The literature on the effects of birth order on children is voluminous, and we cannot do it justice with our admittedly short summary. It does, however, shed considerable light on the personalities, parental influence, and motivation of today's business leaders.

It is often claimed that, on the average, firstborn children are more intelligent than are laterborn children. Some researchers have even gone so far as to claim that the intelligence of each child in a family will be lower than that of the previous one.

Most recent data suggest that the burden of proof still remains with those who assert an impact of birth order on intelligence. Many older studies had failed to control for family size or had equated only children (who do seem to do better in numerous ways) to firstborns, thereby bringing up the average scores of the latter. However, there is some evidence that firstborns are more likely to come out in the highest levels of intelligence, even when studies control for family size. This is supported by studies of highly intelligent children and National Merit Scholars, and also a 1967 study by Bayer which showed greater variability in intelligence for firstborn children.

This pattern recurs when we look at success in general. The ranks of the most successful people are heavily populated with only and firstborn children. For example, 21 of the first 23 U.S. astronauts are firstborn children. The same is true for 55 percent of the members of the United States Supreme Court, and for 66 percent of students in Ivy League colleges in 1980. Firstborns are also overrepresented among top scientists, academicians, doctors, Rhodes Scholars, and persons listed in *Who's Who*. At least one researcher has suggested that firstborns predominate because they attend college in disproportionate numbers. This would accord well with data on proportions of the firstborn in college. To quote another research study on birth order,

> . . . firstborns are overrepresented in college, including graduate programs, and . . . the degree of overrepresentation increases with the level of education involved. The more highly selective the college, the greater the degree of overrepresentation. This varied from over 60 percent in the famous private colleges (Yale, Reed) to around 50 percent in large state colleges compared to some 30 percent to 40 percent of firstborns in the general population.[7]

The Lastborn Do Well, Too

It turns out, however, that it is not only firstborns who are overrepresented in college. The lastborns also attend college in proportions greater than their representation in the general population. As Bayer reported in a study of individuals receiving doctorate degrees, youngest children are underrepresented among two and three children families (which is evident; if the older is overrepresented, the younger must be underrepresented), but in larger families, more doctorates than might be expected are earned by lastborns. Another study by Bayer found that, after only children, firstborn and lastborn children are the most likely to go to college.

Possible Explanations of the High Achievement Levels of Firstborn and Only Children

Numerous explanations have been advanced to account for the superior performance of firstborn (especially only) children and lastborn children, at the expense of middle children. Since there is no evidence for suspecting systematic genetic differences, attention usually focuses on environmental and socialization factors. Sutton-Smith and Rosenberg summarize numerous findings on middleborns, with the conclusion that they are relatively neglected. "They do not get the exclusive attention of being firstborn, or the doting attention of being youngest (at least not for long)." And all the studies on which they report have negative implications for the middle born, showing that they participate in " . . . more negative attention-getting . . . are most changeable . . . are less often given affectionate nicknames by parents . . . and are least popular. . . ."[8]

Mary Ann Gleason, vice president of Atlanta-based Sun Data, Inc., was born third in a family of four. Gleason remembers how upset her parents were when their first child, a daughter, moved out of their home. When Gleason's secondborn brother left, her parents reluctantly agreed that it might be for the best. But when Gleason was considering such a move, her parents announced that they were selling the house, and suggested she should move.

One clear difference in upbringing that exists between firstborn and laterborn children is that parents of firstborns tend to be less sure they are doing things right, since they have no experience on which to rely. After the first child, parents tend to be more relaxed in their child rearing practices. As a result, parents tend to be more demanding with their firstborn. This could be one explanation for the finding that firstborn children show a higher need to achieve than subsequent children. This finding applies, however, only to children from upper- and middle-income brackets. Among lower-income subjects, the youngest children have the highest need to achieve, followed by oldest children, then middle children. Among more affluent families, the oldest child tends to be more driven to succeed than the lastborn (except in two child families), and more driven to succeed than middle children in families of medium size, but, very surprisingly, less driven to succeed than middle children in large families.

Birth Order and Personality

With particular positions in the birth order come certain personality tendencies. Although it goes without saying that these tendencies are not hard and fast predictions of anyone's personality (since there are many other contributing factors), they do capture broad patterns.

Firstborns generally fall into two basic categories. They are either compliant, with a strong desire to please, or they are strong-willed and aggressive. Professional counselor Frank Lombardo describes the second type of firstborn as follows:

> The strong-willed firstborn can be compared to Dr. Craig on the TV series *St. Elsewhere*. He's a very driven person and highly expectant of others, too. The strong-willed firstborn also has a need to be number one in things. Generally, these people have confidence that they'll be taken seriously throughout their lives because they were taken seriously first by their parents. This attributes to their high rate of success in their climbs to the top and is to their advantage. They're also pacesetters in that they set the standards for the rest of the family. This unfortunately puts a lot of pressure on them, and we counselors end up with many firstborns as clients.[9]

Lonely onlies have many of the same traits present in firstborns. In fact, adding the word "super" before each adjective best describes the attributes of only children, attributes which contribute to their demonstrated successes in many walks of life. They are self-assured, and tend to have high self-esteem. They tend to be self-sufficient, and are likely to have spent a great deal of time alone as children. On the other hand, they are not as good in social situations, in negotiating, or in sharing.

Oldest children tend to be supervisors. They acquired early experience watching over their younger siblings. They also became good listeners, giving an ear to both parents and siblings. On the other hand, the eldest are often rule-bound conformists, and they do not like to accept the fact that they might need help sometimes.

Youngest children, as suggested earlier, can be the most ambitious and successful children in a family. They feel more secure than the middle children, and can be innovative problem-solvers. On the downside, they can be self-centered as a result of being spoiled as children, and can be somewhat of a misfit.

The Middle Child Syndrome

Middle children are sometimes thought of as born rebels, and rightfully so. Denied the advantages of the firstborn and the "baby" of the family, middle children will often rebel against family restrictions. On the other hand, they will often accept the dictates of their peer groups. Middle children tend to be fairly insecure and sensitive, but they often have the best social skills in the family.

The Wall Street Journal once described Richard Nixon as a classic middle child. He exhibited his sensitivity after losing the California gubernatorial race, when he angrily told reporters that they would not have him to kick around any more. On the other hand, his diplomatic skills later allowed him to open relations between the United States and the People's Republic of China.

Birth Order of Today's CEOs and Intelligence

Three of every four of today's CEOs are first or secondborn. In addition, a definite relationship exists between their birth order and whether they are stronger in verbal or numerical ability (Table 1–2). Firstborn CEOs are much more balanced between quantitative and verbal ability, with 41 percent saying they are better with quantitative problems, 46 percent rating their verbal ability as better, and 13 percent saying they are equally good at numerical and verbal skills. By contrast, the later the respondent was born, the more likely he is to be oriented toward the verbal side, as the following table shows. Again, note the little surge among lastborns in the increase of the proportion of those stronger in numerical ability than in verbal ability.

Interestingly enough, the CEOs do not seem to reflect the usual trend of the firstborn and lastborn doing the best, at least as far as college grades are concerned. In fact, firstborns had a lower average than those born second, third, or fourth. In fact, they did better only than those born fifth. This is exactly the opposite of what we would expect on the basis of the studies mentioned earlier which showed better grades for the firstborn. Yet, it is indeed the firstborn CEOs who had the highest proportion of "C" averages in college

---

Table 1–2: Birth Order and Numerical and Verbal Abilities

Birth Order	Numerical Abilities	Verbal Abilities	Equal Abilities
First	41%	46%	13%
Second	28	60	10
Third	21	74	6
Fourth	13	75	13
Fifth or later	20	80	0

Table 1–3: Birth Order and College Grades

| Birth Order | Average Grade | | | Overall Grade |
	A	B	C	Point Average
First	38%	51%	8%	3.2
Second	40	52	8	3.3
Third	37	57	3	3.3
Fourth	56	44	—	3.6
Fifth or later	13	87	—	3.1

and the lowest overall averages, while respondents born fourth and later had no averages lower than "As" and "Bs" (Table 1-3).

CEOs' Birth Order and Name Used

As noted earlier, middle children tend to get relatively less attention from their parents than first or lastborn children, and one aspect of this is that they are less likely to receive a nickname from their parents. The later a CEO was born, the more likely it is that he uses his first name as opposed to his middle name, initials, or nickname. However, practically every CEO goes by his first name or a nickname; the use of a middle name or initials is uncommon. The only exceptions to this are those who were first or secondborn and who, to some extent, do use their middle names. T. Boone Pickens, Jr. is an example. Pickens, a lonely only, has remarked:

> My name was always a problem. My mother was afraid if they called me T. Boone, it would come out T-Bone. Also, I was a timid kid, and because people confused Boone with Ben and other names, I wanted to change it to Tom. But my mother said, "Stick with it, son. Someday you won't have any problem telling people who you are."[10]

The CEO data tend to support the generalization that middle born children are less likely to be given affectionate nicknames. The chart below provides clear evidence of the tendency of parents to refer to their middle children by their first names. Fully one-third of all firstborn CEOs use a nickname; only about one-fifth of secondborns do. By contrast, almost two-thirds of all youngest children use a nickname (Table 1–4).

Table 1–4: Birth Order and Name Used

	Birth Order			
Name Used	First-born	Second-born	Third-born	Fourth-born or Later
First name	51%	58%	65%	26%
Middle name	11	8	—	13
Nickname	33	21	29	63
Initials	3	3	3	—
First & initials or nickname	1	3	—	—
Middle & initials or nickname	1	5	—	—

Note: Totals may not add to 100 percent due to rounding.

SUMMING UP

The data gathered on the family backgrounds of chief executive officers provide numerous insights about how these corporate leaders grew up. In the first place, today's CEOs were born largely in what today is called the Rust Belt. With the exceptions of Texas and California, the high-growth states of the Sunbelt have yet to supply large numbers of chief executive officers. A little over 4 percent of CEOs were born abroad.

Families have changed significantly since today's CEOs were born. Eighty-eight percent of CEOs grew up in two-parent households, and in most cases their mothers did not hold a job outside the household. Nowadays, less than 60 percent of all households are headed by two adults, and over 50 percent of all married women work outside the home. CEOs from rich and very poor backgrounds are the most likely to come from two-parent households (100 percent), while only about 85 percent of middle class and upper-lower class CEOs grew up in two-parent families.

Another change that has occurred since today's CEOs were growing up is that family size has decreased. More families have no children (49 percent), and the families that do have children are having fewer children than the CEOs' generation. This can clearly be seen when the size of the families in which the CEOs grew up (an average of 2.9 children) is compared with the average today (1.8 children) for those families with children. In particular, there are very few only children among current CEOs (12 percent), compared with about 42 percent of only children in today's families. When family size is analyzed in terms of social class, we find that the CEOs who came from a rich or a very poor background did not grow up as only children; and their families tended, in general, to have had more children than did middle class and upper-lower class families. Thus, we find the same split among classes on both number of parents and number of children: the rich and the very poor had two parents, and more children than average.

Data collected on the CEOs' birth order tend to confirm most of the generalizations about birth order reported in earlier studies. For example, 44 percent of today's CEOs are only children or firstborns, which confirms studies showing a general overrepresentation of firstborns among the eminent. This is especially clear when one considers that the proportion of firstborns was lower in their generation than it is today. Firstborn CEOs are almost evenly divided between superiority at verbal or quantitative skills, while those born later are much more likely to excel at verbal rather than numerical ability. One finding that contradicts earlier studies is that firstborn CEOs tended to do slightly worse in college in terms of grades than those born second through fourth, but better than those born fifth or later. Finally, middleborn children who became CEOs were less likely to receive affectionate nicknames, and there is a substantially lower percentage of second- and thirdborns who use a nickname than first and fourth (or later) born CEOs.

In terms of family background, then, a small number of characteristics stand out for today's CEOs in comparison with the general population. They grew up in larger families and were more likely to have both parents present than is common today. They are also more likely to be firstborn. But to uncover more details concerning what makes CEOs different from other men and women, we must look to other factors.

—————■—————

1. John A. Byrne, "Fathers and Sons," *Forbes,* 28 January 1985, 94-95.
2. Sherrye Henry, "How They Began," *Parade Magazine,* 1 February 1987, 5.
3. Part of this chapter is based on an article by the authors. See "Parental Influence and Family Size as Variables Shaping CEO Careers," *Review of Business,* Summer 1987, 9-12. Used by permission of St. John University.
4. Marilyn A. Harris, Zachery Schiller, Russell Mitchell, and Christopher Power, "Can Jack Welch Reinvent GE?" *Business Week,* 30 June 1986, 62-67.
5. Anthony Branco, "Jerry Tsai: The Comeback Kid," *Business Week,* 18 August 1986, 72-78.
6. Fern Schumer Chapman, "Executive Guilt: Who's Taking Care of the Children?" *Fortune,* 16 February 1987, 31-32.
7. "Birth Order and Intelligence," *Science News,* 27 March 1982, 218.
8. Brian Sutton-Smith and B. G. Rosenberg, *The Sibling* (New York: Holt, Rinehart and Winston, 1970).
9. Leesa Bolling, "Whoever Comes First is Neither Best Nor Worst," *Mobile Press,* 29 January 1987, 17A.
10. Henry, 5.

"Happy is the child whose father died rich."

Proverb

2

SOCIAL CLASS

Over a decade ago, the editors of *Fortune* magazine decided
to determine, once and for all, whether the chief executive
suite was the exclusive domain of the rich and their off-
spring. Their survey of *Fortune* 500 CEOs led them to conclude that this belief was a myth:

> One of the hoariest myths about the top corporate officer is
> that he comes primarily from a wealthy or at least upper-
> middle-class background, and thus has a special advantage in
> getting to the top. There may have been a grain of truth to the
> idea in years past, but the backgrounds of today's chief execu-
> tives suggest that the notion is now thoroughly obsolete.[1]

Portia Isaacson never needed a survey to convince herself
that this belief is a myth. Isaacson, CEO of numerous computer software firms including Future Computing Inc. and
Intellisys Corporation, grew up dirt-poor in a broken home
on an Oklahoma dairy farm. Socially ostracized in high
school because of her poverty, and hating her stepmother,
she left home with $25 in her pocket the same day she
graduated as valedictorian of her high school class. Her
career has included stints at Xerox and Electronic Data
Systems, a marriage and three sons, and a Ph.D. in computer science from Southern Methodist University.[2]

But is Isaacson the exception to the rule? In this chapter, we examine the social backgrounds of today's chief
executive officers, particularly the social classes in which
they grew up.

LET'S DEFINE SOME TERMS

"Class" is one of those terms so loaded with connotations that it is necessary to listen closely to anyone using it to understand the intended meaning. As publisher Malcolm Forbes puts it, "People's wealth and worth are very rarely related."[3] In our usage of the term, we will follow the well-known Warner social class hierarchy as updated by Yale sociologist Richard P. Coleman, which divides American society into the following six categories:

Upper-upper class. The top stratum is comprised of socially prominent families having old (usually inherited) money—the true "preppies" who send their children to Ivy League colleges.

Lower-upper class. This is made up of the "nouveau riche," the elite of numerous sectors of society who have earned their wealth rather than inherited it. Many of those involved at the highest echelons in business and government would be categorized as lower-upper.

Upper-middle class. This stratum is comprised of corporate management, owners of medium-sized businesses, and professionals such as physicians and successful attorneys. College backgrounds are typical for these people.

Lower-middle class. This category includes white-collar workers, small business owners, and socially ambitious blue-collar families with better than average educations.

Upper-lower or working class. This is largely made up of blue-collar and service workers. Incomes vary widely, and high school educations are typical.

Lower-lower class. These primarily unskilled or semi-skilled workers are sometimes unemployed, sometimes on welfare.

This classification system, which has been used in a variety of sociological, behavioral, and marketing studies over the years, is now the most widely accepted description of social classes in the United States. The Warner-Coleman categories are an ideal basis for analyzing the social backgrounds of our CEOs.

DIVERSE BACKGROUNDS
CHARACTERIZE OUR CEOs

Although CEOs take different routes to the top, their career paths are similar in that they are affected heavily by the circumstances in which they grew up. Consider the following examples.

Roy Park of Park Communications grew up as a farm boy in a poor family. He excelled in school and showed a flair for writing at an early age. He was 15 years old when he entered North Carolina State University and financed his education by writing for the Associated Press. After graduating from college, he turned his energies toward public relations and advertising, but after 17 years made a sharp turn and went into the cake mix business as founder of Duncan Hines. Later, when the firm was merged into Procter and Gamble, he returned to media and bought radio and television stations as well as newspapers. Today, his empire contains seven TV stations, 14 radio stations, 25 daily papers, and 50 other publications.

Malcolm McLean of McLean Industries was the son of a mail carrier. After graduating from high school, he ran a gas station and bought a used truck from which emerged McLean Trucking. During his years in the trucking business, he developed the idea of cargo containerization. Eventually his interests expanded into real estate and agribusiness and, in 1978, he acquired U.S. Lines, the core of McLean Industries.

Milton Petrie of Petrie Stores came from a typical lower-middle class family. His father owned a pawnshop, but eventually went broke. Petrie had a checkered career, opening his first clothing store in 1927 and expanding throughout the 1930s until he went bankrupt in 1937. He didn't let this stop him for long; he started over again, and now has over 1,300 women's specialty stores with annual sales of over $600 million. He has accomplished at least part of this by being somewhat of a takeover artist, specializing in the acquisition of other clothing stores.

Claude Pennington of Pennington Oil Company was the son of a doctor who ran an eye and ear clinic. He, too, started out as an optometrist. At age 30 he stopped practicing medicine to work in the oil and natural gas fields of his native Louisiana and surrounding states. He worked "seven days a week, including Christmas," and hit it big with a major discovery in 1952. Now worth over $200 million, "Doc" Pennington drills about 75 wells each year.

Robert Galvin, the only son of Motorola founder Paul Galvin, was destined to follow in his father's footsteps. Heading the firm in the 1960s, he diversified Motorola—which had specialized in car radios and television sets—into a general communications company. During this time he also extended Motorola worldwide.

HOW TYPICAL ARE THE BACKGROUNDS OF AMERICA'S CEOs?

The question of the social backgrounds of America's business leaders is part of a larger debate concerning the nature of American society. Simply put, the question is whether a small, elite group of society in one way or another controls key public decisions, as charged by critics such as G. William Domhoff and the late C. Wright Mills. One aspect of this debate is the issue of social mobility, including the absence of a dynastic business elite in the United States.

Early Research on the Subject

A seminal work on the question of the existence of a business elite was published in 1955 by Mabel Newcomer, chair of Vassar's Department of Economics, Sociology, and Anthropology. *The Big Business Executive*, which looked at both chairmen and presidents of corporations, differed slightly from our survey data base; but it provides the best comparative information available on the background of corporate leaders from 1900 to 1950.

For 1900, Newcomer found that almost 46 percent of chairmen and presidents came from wealthy backgrounds, about 42 percent from middle class backgrounds, and 12 percent from poor families. By 1925, the proportion of top officers who grew up rich had fallen to 36 percent, the middle class had raised its share to nearly 48 percent, and the lower economic classes supplied 16 percent of presidents and chairmen. By 1950, the proportion of those with wealthy backgrounds in top spots was largely unchanged, while the number of middle class leaders had increased to almost 52 percent, and the number from poor families had fallen to 12 percent. Table 2–1 summarizes these findings.

A 1976 *Fortune* survey expanded the Newcomer data by adding information drawn from a survey of the CEOs of *Fortune* 500 companies. It revealed a sharp decline in the proportion of CEOs who came from wealthy backgrounds, and a concomitant increase in the number who came from middle class families. In particular, a greater proportion of CEOs came from lower-middle class backgrounds than from the upper-middle class. The *Fortune* study considered this to be part of the general post-World War II trend toward greater mobility. Table 2–2 summarizes these findings.

Table 2–1: Social Class Rankings of the Parents of CEOs: 1900 to 1950

	Percentage of CEOs		
Economic Class	1900	1925	1950
Rich	46%	36%	36%
Middle	42	48	52
Poor	12	16	12

Source: Reprinted from Mabel Newcomer, *The Big Business Executive*, (New York: Columbia University Press, 1955)

Table 2–2: Social Class Rankings of the Parents of CEOs: 1950

Economic Class	Percentage of CEOs
Upper	6%
Upper–middle	41
Lower–middle	43
Poor	9

Source: Adapted from Charles G. Burck, "A Group Profile of the Fortune 500 Chief Executive," *Fortune* (May, 1976), p. 174. ©1976, Time Inc., all rights reserved.

Backgrounds of Today's CEOs Differ from Earlier Times

Our data show somewhat different results from those of the earlier studies, but confirm the general trend toward a greater representation of middle class backgrounds among the CEOs of America's top corporations.[4] Table 2–3 illustrates the class breakdown of American society as a whole and the family backgrounds of today's CEOs.

These figures not only indicate that almost two-thirds of today's CEOs come from well-off backgrounds in general, but also that the top three classes are highly overrepresented (a ratio more than 4 times their presence in the general population). It is also somewhat surprising that there is more "old money" than "new money" in the CEOs' backgrounds; as a consequence, the lower-upper class is overrepresented among CEOs only by a factor of about 3.

It can also be seen that there is a grain of truth to the "hoariest of myths"—that the top echelons of American business are dominated by those who have an advantage in getting there because they come from wealthier families. Unlike the *Fortune* study, we found that the top rank of America's corporations is dominated by those from the

Table 2–3: Social Class and National Statistics

Social Class	Percentage of All Americans	Percentage of CEOs
Upper-upper	less than 1%	4%
Lower-upper	1	4
Upper-middle	13	56
Lower-middle	32	18
Upper-lower	38	16
Lower-lower	16	2

upper-middle class rather than the lower-middle class. Instead of a rough equality between upper-middle and lower-middle class backgrounds, we found the percentage of CEOs coming from the upper-middle class to be about three times higher than from the lower-middle class.

A COMPARISON OF SOCIAL CLASSES BY INDUSTRY

To develop a better understanding of the CEOs' class backgrounds, the CEOs were categorized by industry group, and the social background of each group was examined separately. Wide disparities among industry groups were found, as represented in the industry-by-industry comparison in Table 2–4.

Interesting Differences Exist by Industry

A number of interesting observations can be made using the information in Table 2–4. First, the industry that most

Table 2–4: Social Class and Industry

Industry	Social Class		
	Upper	Middle	Lower
Manufacturing	4%	81%	15%
Banking	11	73	16
Utilities	2	67	31
Retailing	18	71	12
Wholesaling	—	80	20
Service industries	7	83	10
Food products	18	82	—
Medical products	—	75	25
Transportation	—	89	11
All CEOs	8	75	17

closely mirrors the overall distribution of social backgrounds is manufacturing—not surprising since it has the second largest pool of respondents. Banking is also fairly close to the overall averages; though, in what may be a surprise to many, it has the largest percentage of CEOs from lower-lower class backgrounds.

One large industry—utilities—clearly stands out from the others. Not only does it have far fewer CEOs from upper-middle class backgrounds than does the sample as a whole, it also has only one upper-upper class CEO, which easily makes it the industry whose CEOs had the humblest beginnings. In particular, the utilities industry has the highest proportion of upper-lower class respondents.

Wholesaling has the highest percentage of lower-middle class CEOs, with 40 percent. At the other end of the income spectrum, retailing has the highest percentage of CEOs who grew up with upper-upper class backgrounds.

Retailing is not the richest overall industry, however; that distinction should go to the food products industry, in which almost 91 percent of the CEOs grew up in upper-middle class or richer households. It has the highest proportion of CEOs of both lower-upper and upper-middle class backgrounds: 9 percent and 73 percent respectively.

THE LINK BETWEEN
SOCIAL CLASS AND EDUCATION

Analysis of data on the CEOs' high school and college educations not only provided information about their schooling, but also allowed us to have more confidence in the answers they gave about the social backgrounds in which they grew up.

Secondary School Attendance Verifies Our Data

Information about high school in particular helped validate responses about social class. A clear relationship was found between class and the type of high school the respondent attended. Had there not been such a relationship, i.e., if large numbers of respondents of the lower class had gone to private high schools, the analysis would have shown the existence of high rates of romanticizing by CEOs about their childhood social classes. Indeed, it would have made it very difficult, if not impossible, to identify trends in the social backgrounds of America's business leaders due to a lack of reliable information on their backgrounds. Fortunately, the CEOs did not show overly romantic views of their childhoods, probably due to our construction of class definitions in terms of "father's occupation." As a result of the survey's structure, a close relationship was established between social class and high school education, as Table 2–5 shows.

The chart indicates that the lower classes were more likely to attend a public high school than were those from

Table 2–5: Social Class and Secondary School Attended

| | Type of Secondary School | | |
Social Class	Public	Private	Both
Upper-upper	20%	70%	10%
Lower-upper	25	75	
Upper-middle	78	17	5
Lower-middle	91	9	
Upper-lower	91	9	
Lower-lower	100		

higher social classes. The sharp increase from lower-upper class to upper-middle class suggests the accuracy of the CEOs' self-assessments of their social class backgrounds.

The Relationship Between Social Class and College Attended

The types of colleges the CEOs attended also confirm the information given on social classes and high school backgrounds. Considering all classes, the study revealed that not all of today's CEOs went to Ivy League colleges; though, of course, they were more likely to have done so than the average American. It was found that CEOs were much more likely than the average person to have attended and graduated from college. While only about one of three Americans has completed at least one year of college, and only one of six has earned a degree, 99 percent of CEOs attended college and 91 percent graduated. (See Chapter 7 for more details.)

Also interesting is that, with the exception of CEOs who grew up in lower-lower class families, they were far more likely to have gone to a private college or university than to

Table 2–6: Social Class and College Attended

Social Class	Type of College		
	Public	**Ivy League**	**Other Private**
Upper-upper	10%	30%	50%
Lower-upper	25	63	25
Upper-middle	43	20	44
Lower-middle	58	9	45
Upper-lower	63	9	40
Lower-lower	75	—	—

Note: Totals sometimes do not add to 100 percent because of multiple college attendance and nonresponses.

have attended a private high school. Table 2–6 shows these results.

Again, a clear relationship can be seen between the class background of the CEO and the type of college attended. The less well-off the future CEO was, the more likely he was to attend a public college or university. Interestingly, the survey shows that future CEOs from a lower-upper class background were the most likely to "go Ivy," even over those from upper-upper class backgrounds. Another interesting point is that respondents coming from the upper- and lower-middle classes and from the upper-lower class were the most likely to have attended several different types of colleges—over 10 percent in each case.

College Funding Is Linked to Social Class Data

The final aspect of social class studied was the question of how CEOs financed their educations. CEOs were asked to indicate all sources of funding for their college educations. As expected, a clear relationship exists between the

Table 2-7: Collegiate Parental-Funding and Social Class

Social Class	Percentage of CEOs With Parental Support
Upper-upper	70%
Lower-upper	88
Upper-middle	65
Lower-middle	42
Upper-lower	17
Lower-lower	—

respondent's social background and how his college education was financed. This relationship is most clearly
reflected in the percentage of future CEOs whose college
educations were financed by their parents. Table 2-7 shows
the percentage of respondents from each class whose parents contributed to their educations.

Except that parents of lower-upper class respondents
were more likely to pay for college than were parents of
upper-upper class students, this table shows a very straightforward relationship between class and whether the parents
paid for school. There are no surprises here.

Other sources of college funding more easily controlled
by the students included part-time and full-time jobs and/
or scholarships. (When today's CEOs were in college, the
federal student loan program did not exist.) The results of
the study are somewhat different from what might be
expected. Table 2-8 shows the percentage of future CEOs
who provided either part or all of the cost of their college
educations through their own resources.

Several things are interesting in this table. First, note
that less than 15 percent of all upper and middle class
future CEOs paid all of their college costs. It is surprising

Table 2–8: Collegiate Self-Funding and Social Class

Social Class	Partial Self-Payment	Full Self-Payment
Upper-upper	—	—
Lower-upper	25%	13%
Upper-middle	53	10
Lower-middle	71	13
Upper-lower	40	46
Lower-lower	50	50

that a higher proportion of lower-upper class future chief executives did so than did upper-middle class students, but this difference is not very large. Also, note that although lower class future CEOs exhibited the highest rate of total self-payment, the peak rate of partial self-financing came from the lower-middle class rather than from lower class future executives. However, as Table 2–9 shows, it is not because CEOs from lower class backgrounds received more scholarships. In fact, lower-middle class background CEOs comprised the highest proportion of scholarship recipients. There were no scholarship recipients among our survey participants who grew up in a wealthy background.

SUMMING UP

In our search for the reasons why some business people get to the top echelon of American corporations, we found that social class plays a definite role. While there may not be a hereditary elite of business leaders, there is no question that the majority of our top business leaders came from relatively privileged positions in society.

Table 2–9: Collegiate Scholarship and Social Class

Social Class	Percentage of CEOs Receiving Scholarships
Upper-upper	—
Lower-upper	—
Upper-middle	23%
Lower-middle	53
Upper-lower	26
Lower-lower	50

Our data show the rich and the upper-middle classes are overrepresented among American CEOs by a considerable margin. However, it is not usually the children of the rich who rise to the top positions in the largest American corporations—though certainly many of them do. Most commonly, it is the children of the professional, upper-middle class who provide America with its business leadership. Comprising just over 50 percent of all CEOs, the upper-middle class appears to be the jumping-off point for further social mobility. This finding contradicts a key conclusion of a 1976 *Fortune* study that most CEOs come from lower-middle class backgrounds. On the other hand, it should be recalled that the data on CEOs' fathers' occupations suggest that the change in the social backgrounds of America's CEOs from childhood to the present may not be as great as it appears in the raw data on social class, which is more subjective and more open to romanticism.

Another important finding of our study is that there are divergences among industries as related to the social backgrounds of their CEOs. Among the industries most open to CEOs from lower class backgrounds are utilities, manufacturing and, surprisingly, banking. Indeed, banking has the highest proportion of CEOs from lower-lower class backgrounds. Among the preserves of the wealthy are retailing, which has the highest percentage of upper-upper class CEOs, and food products, with the highest combined percentage of upper- and lower-upper class background respondents, as well as the highest proportion of lower-upper class respondents. In addition, food products has the highest share of upper-middle class executives, making it the most concentrated of all industries toward the top three classes. Wholesaling, service industries, medical products, and transportation comprise the bastion of the middle classes, as all four industries draw their CEOs almost exclusively from the middle classes and upper-lower class.

Finally, clear and straightforward relationships exist between the CEOs' social backgrounds while growing up and the educations they received, as well as the likelihood of schooling being paid for by their parents or by themselves. Whatever their social backgrounds, future CEOs helped pave the way for their eventual climbs to the top by working hard in both high school and college and getting as much out of their educations as possible.

1. Charles G. Burck, "A Group Portrait of the Fortune 500 Chief Executives," *Fortune*, May 1976, 173-77.
2. Thomas R. Horton, *What Works For Me* (New York: Random House, 1986), 302, 308.
3. Malcolm Forbes, *The Sayings of Chairman Malcolm* (New York: Harper & Row, 1978), 79.
4. Some of this material appeared in an earlier article by the authors. See "The Road to the Top," *American Demographics*, March 1988, 34–37. Used by permission.

WOULD YOU CALL
THIS MAN
GOOD-LOOKING?

*"I don't know if people consider me good-looking
or not . . . you guys can decide."*

Robert J. Harrison, CEO
Public Service Company of
New Hampshire

3

PERSONAL CHARACTERISTICS

Robert Harrison's response to our question on whether people consider him attractive illustrates the humor of our CEOs. (For the record, Mrs. Harrison says her husband is an extremely good-looking man.) This same question sparked other examples of humor. 3M CEO Lewis W. Lehr asked "two close associates" to answer the question; they stated that they did not know if Mr. Lehr was good-looking. One can only wonder if these people are still close associates. That may depend on Lehr's sense of humor. As *Forbes* publisher Malcolm Forbes put it, "To be good-looking is a handicap, it's often said—usually by those who aren't."[1]

An extensive research study conducted at Chicago's Rush Medical College identified several personal characteristics that affect one's advancement in the corporate world. Everything from height to sense of humor—or the lack of one—plays a role in how well one does in business. In this chapter, we examine a number of personal characteristics of today's CEOs in our search for additional clues about what makes a chief executive officer tick.

DO CEOs HAVE A SENSE OF HUMOR?

Dullness, or as the Rush researchers call it, "low pleasure capacity," is a good starting point for discussing humor. They found that the fun-lovers in their survey of 88 executives tended to earn less, complain more, and have fewer on-the-job responsibilities. According to survey director David C. Clark, this group may be reacting to workplace stress by seeking fun after work.

A contradictory view is offered by Howard Pullio, Distinguished Professor of Psychology at the University of Tennessee, who has studied humor extensively. Pullio considers humor essential for managerial success. He comments, "The higher up the corporate ladder you climb, the more of a sense of humor you're allowed to have. On your way up, it's nose to the grindstone. But once you make it, you're expected to have grand wit."[2]

The Authors Offer an Opinion

Although we did not specifically measure "pleasure capacity," we did ask CEOs whether their friends and family thought they had a good sense of humor, certainly one facet of dullness or its opposite. Our findings tend to disaffirm the Rush Medical College results. A clear majority (60 percent) report that their family and friends think they are humorous. Another 35 percent are considered by others as having a moderate sense of humor. Only one in 20 says others view him as humorless.

In his book, *Augustine's Law*, Norman R. Augustine describes an event that would only be possible with a CEO who was well-known for his sense of humor. This particular CEO had fallen ill and was recuperating in a local hospital. A messenger delivered to the CEO's bedside a copy of a resolution by the firm's board of directors wishing him a speedy return to work—on which the corporate secretary had dutifully, albeit indiscreetly, recorded "Approved by a vote of 6 to 4."[3]

We can conclude—if self-reporting has not distorted the data—that the humorless do not often make it to the top of corporate America. One qualification is in order, however; the Rush conclusions may be true for a wide range of middle-level executive positions.

AGE PATTERNS AMONG CEOs

The median age of America's CEOs has increased considerably during the twentieth century. In 1900, the figure stood at 53 years, meaning that half of all corporate leaders were younger than 53. By 1976, the median age had increased to 57.

Today's CEOs have a median age of 58. In comparing current CEO age distributions with those of a decade ago, we find a general tendency toward older chief executives. One in 16 CEOs is 65 or older today. By contrast, only one in 33 was this old a decade ago. At the other end of the age spectrum, only half as many CEOs are under 45 today as in 1976. A decade ago, almost 2 percent of all CEOs were under 40. But these ultra-fast track individuals have not been followed by a new generation of young corporate leaders, and as CEOs like Fred Smith of Federal Express have reached the 40-year-old plateau, no CEO of a major corporation is today under 40. Table 3–1 shows the changes in the various CEO age brackets over the past decade.

Not only has there been a general increase in the average age of CEOs, but some changes are particularly marked. The 50 to 54 age group shows the largest change. Ten years ago, there were almost as many in this group as in the 60- to 64-year-old group. More recently, there were only half as many.

THE QUESTION OF HEIGHT

A certain mystique surrounds height, and there is little question that a person's height influences how well he does

Table 3–1: Changes in CEO Age Distributions Since 1976

Age	1976 CEO Age Distribution	Current CEO Age Distribution
65 and older	3%	6%
55 to 64	60	68
45 to 54	33	26
44 or younger	4	2

Note: Totals may not add to 100 percent due to rounding.

in life. As examples of some of the effects of height on a person's career, Ralph Keyes cites studies showing that annual salaries for men increase $250 per inch between 5'6" and 5'11," with a further increase of $1,500 for the next two inches. Business aside, shorter men find it harder to get dates because most women prefer dating someone taller than they are. But men, Keyes says, enjoy having shorter male friends.

Keyes suggests that businesses prefer taller men in executive positions, citing a study by this book's co-author Kurtz in which 140 sales managers tended to choose the taller of two equally-qualified job candidates. Short people, though, seem to have done well as entrepreneurs. Andrew Carnegie and Ray Kroc are examples.

The Determinants of Height

The determinants of height comprise an interesting issue. Richard H. Steckel, in a study for the National Bureau of Economic Research, surveyed data on the average height of adults and adolescents for 20 countries worldwide. Steckel sought to discover the main determinants of a nation's average height. His statistical analysis confirmed the established wisdom that environment has more to do with adult height than does heredity. Interestingly, he found that for adolescents, ethnic descent was often a factor in determining height. But these effects all disappeared with adulthood. For adults, what mattered was the individual's sex (no surprise), the country's per capita income, and income distribution. Income works its effects through nutrition and access to health care. The more equal the distribution of income in a society, the greater will be the population's average height, since more people will have adequate nutrition and access to health care to reach their full genetic potentials.

CEO Height

Although today's CEOs reach both extremes in height— from 6'6" Charles Harper of Con Agra to 5'4" Dwayne Orville Andreas of Archer—the height data shown in Table 3–2 suggest the effect of income at work. Recall from the previous chapter that a clear majority of today's CEOs came from an upper-middle class or wealthy background; then consider the information on height shown below.

Table 3–2: Height Distribution of CEOs

Height	Percentage
5'7" and under	2%
5'8" to 5'9"	8
5'10" to 5'11"	30
6'0" to 6'1"	32
6'2" to 6'3"	18
6'4" and over	10

Three of every five CEOs are at least six feet tall. By contrast, the average height for American men is only about 5'9." In other words, almost 90 percent of today's CEOs are taller than the average male. Actually, the percentage is even higher when CEOs are compared with people their own age, because average height has been increasing in the United States. For example, in the 55- to 64-year-old age group, which contains two-thirds of all CEOs, the average height of U.S. males is only 5'8," while for those 65 and over, the average U.S. male's height is only 5'7."

PLEASE STEP ON THE SCALE

Keeping trim is a way of life for most CEOs. For some, like T. Boone Pickens, Jr. of Mesa Petroleum, this means strict adherence to a spartan regimen. The 5'9" Pickens consumes about 2,000 calories a day. He counts calories every day, and once he tips the scales at 165 pounds he starts cutting calories. To help maintain his weight, Pickens jogs and plays racquetball. Table 3–3 shows the weight patterns of America's CEOs.

Table 3–3: Weight Distribution of CEOs

Weight	Percentage
150 lbs. or less	5%
151 to 160 lbs.	8
161 to 170 lbs.	12
171 to 180 lbs.	18
181 to 190 lbs.	21
191 to 200 lbs.	17
201 to 210 lbs.	8
211 to 220 lbs.	5
221 to 230 lbs.	3
231 lbs. or more	3

Only one in five CEOs exceeds Metropolitan Life's widely-used standard for large-frame males by more than 10 pounds. These standards are based on the Build and Blood Pressure Study conducted by the Society of Actuaries. (This contrasts with 67 percent of the book's authors who exceed the standard used above.)

SOUTHPAWS VERSUS RIGHTIES

It is widely believed that the functional organization of the brain is directly associated with which hand a person uses to do most things. For left-handers, the right hemisphere of the brain is dominant; for right-handers, the left hemisphere is dominant. The significance here is that the right side of the brain controls the more analytical, intellectual functions, and the left side is associated with the artistic and similar functions. Another difference is that left-handed people generally can do more things with their right hands than righties can do with their left.

Left-handers are often discriminated against in our society, as they are in most others. The Latin word for left is *sinister* (certainly appropriate for lefties Jack the Ripper and the Boston Strangler), and the French word is *gauche*, also with an obvious negative connotation. Parents and penmanship teachers frequently try to steer children away from writing with their left hands. Many consumer products are designed for right-handers, usable only with difficulty by lefties. Despite the fact that 9 to 12 percent of the population is left-handed (and about another 8 percent potentially so, according to Lefthanders International), many of these items are not duplicated in left-handed versions.

Left-handers are overrepresented by a 2 to 1 margin among gifted math students. Yet about 10 percent of them have developmental problems as a child. So, in many respects, southpaws (a term coined by a Chicago sportswriter in 1890 when he noticed that a left-handed pitcher threw from the south side of the ballpark) like co-author

Boone are different from the right-handed majority of the population.

Compared with the general population, CEOs are more likely to be right-handed. Only 7 percent are left-handed and another 1 percent are ambidextrous. The latter category includes J. W. McLean of Liberty National Corporation (now Banks of Mid-America), John G. Slonecker of Ohio Casualty Corporation, and Arthur O. Sulzberger of the New York Times Company. The CEOs listed in Table 3–4 join the ranks of the lefties who have made their mark in history, including Leonardo da Vinci, Benjamin Franklin, Babe Ruth, Pablo Picasso, Ronald Reagan, Raphael, Charlie Chaplin, and Clarence Darrow.

Since CEOs are overwhelmingly likely to be right-handed, does this mean that they—like other right-handers—tend to be more creative in their problem solving? Maybe so, but this evidence is too slim to warrant that conclusion.

Table 3–4: Left-handed CEOs

Name	Company
Wilson M. Brown, Jr.	Centran Corp. and Central National Bank
James H.C. Duncan	First of America Bank Corporation
James A. Elkins, Jr.	First City of Texas Bancorporation
Charles E. Exley, Jr.	NCR Corporation
Thomas Flynn Faught, Jr.	Dravo Corporation
Robert J. Harrison	Public Service Company of New Hampshire
Robert Dean Hunsucker	Panhandle Eastern Corporation
Abraham Krasnoff	Pall Corporation
Richard Gordon McGovern	Campbell Soup Company
Jerry D. Metcalf	S.M. Flickinger Co., Inc.
James Fischer Montgomery	Great Western Financial Services
John Doyl Ong	The B.F. Goodrich Co.
Lewis T. Preston	Morgan Guaranty Trust Company
David M. Roderick	USX Corporation
John D. Selby	Consumers Power Company
Richard Frank Walker	Public Service Co. of Colorado

An Industry-by-Industry Classification

Comparisons of left- and right-handed CEOs in various industry groups show substantial variation among different industries. Both retailing and medical products show 100 percent right-handers, while wholesaling has the highest proportion (20 percent) of southpaws. Table 3–5 presents the details.

The wholesaling and banking industries (the latter by only a slight margin) have percentages of left-handers that exceed the national average. Utilities, food products, and transportation are within the range defining the national average.

Table 3–5: Hand Usage and Industry Groups

Industry	Right	Left	Ambidextrous
Retailing	100%	—	—
Medical products	100	—	—
Service industries	92.7	9.1%	2.4%
Manufacturing	92.6	7.4	—
Food products	90.9	9.1	—
Transportation	90.9	9.1	—
Utilities	90.7	9.3	—
Banking	85.5	12.7	1.8
Wholesaling	80	20	—

Note: Totals may not add to 100 percent due to multiple responses.

Few Social Class Differences Exist

Only a few surprises appear when CEO handedness is compared along social class lines. First, the lower the social class background in which the CEO grew up, the greater is the likelihood that he is right-handed. Perhaps this is due to a difference in child rearing, in that lower class parents were more likely to prevent their children from writing with their left hands. Equally evident from Table 3–6 is the fact that the only ambidextrous respondents are from the top three classes. This could be accounted for in the same way.

Table 3–6: Hand Usage and Social Class

Social Class Background	Right	Left	Ambidextrous
Upper-upper	80%	10%	10%
Lower-upper	87	—	13
Upper-middle	90	9	1
Lower-middle	91	9	—
Upper-lower	91	9	—
Lower-lower	100	—	—

THE NAME OF THE GAME

Both friends and employees refer to James Robert Moffett, chairman and CEO of Freeport-McMoRan, Inc., as Jim Bob. It's a nickname based on a Texas tradition. Moffett was reared in Texas, where you're virtually always called Jim Bob if your name is James Robert. If Moffett's son, James, Jr., follows in his father's footsteps, we may see a chief executive referred to as Bubba since, according to another Texas tradition, a Jim Bob, Jr., is nicknamed Bubba.

Whatever the reason or tradition, almost three of every 10 CEOs say they go by a nickname. As Table 3–7 shows, nearly half of them go by' a name other than their first name.

Table 3–7: What CEOs Call Themselves

Name Used	Percentage
First	56%
Middle	7
Nickname	29
Initials	3
First initials or first nickname	1
Middle initials or middle nickname	2
No response	2

ARE CEOs A HANDSOME LOT?

As George Orwell put It, "At age 50, every man has the face he deserves."[4] When asked whether other people considered them physically attractive compared to their peers, almost two-thirds of the CEOs answered in the affirmative, a sure sign of a positive self-image and self-confidence. Slightly more than one-third—perhaps the more modest— said they didn't know, and only 2 percent thought other people find them unattractive.

A Link Exists Between Height and Attractiveness

In analyzing our data on physical attractiveness and height, we found a strong tendency for the taller chief executive officers to be more likely to think that others find them attractive.

The results shown in Table 3–8 confirm the idea that short people are disadvantaged relative to tall people. It is clear that, in this sample, short people do not have as positive a self-image as tall people.

Table 3–8: Taller CEOs Think Themselves Attractive

| Height | Attractiveness | | | |
	Yes	No	Don't Know	No Response
5'7" and under	40%	20%	40%	—
5'8" to 5'9"	59	—	35	6%
5'10" to 5'11"	58	—	42	—
6'0" to 6'1"	61	2	36	1
6'2" to 6'3"	71	5	24	—
6'4" and over	71	—	29	—

No Link to Social Class Exists

Despite the correlations between height and the perception of attractiveness and between height and income, we find little relation between social class and attractiveness, as Table 3–9 illustrates.

Table 3–9: Attractiveness Self-Perceptions and Social Class

Social Class	Yes	No	Don't Know	No Response
Upper-upper	50%	—	50%	—
Lower-upper	100	—	—	—
Upper-middle	61	2	36	1
Lower-middle	60	—	40	—
Upper-lower	54	3	40	3
Lower-lower	75	—	25	—

The highest and lowest percentages of "yes" answers are in lower-upper and upper-upper social class backgrounds, respectively. The upper-lower class has the highest percentage of CEOs regarding themselves as unattractive.

An Industry-by-Industry Response Comparison

Some patterns arise between physical attractiveness and industry. None of the CEOs in the medical products industry think others find them attractive; but this is from a very small group comprised of only four respondents. Of the industries with larger numbers of respondents, retailing and service industries both have three times the average proportion of executives who consider themselves unattractive. In fact, these three industries are the only ones with CEOs who rate themselves unattractive. Table 3–10 shows the relationships.

Table 3–10: Attractiveness Self-Perceptions and Industry

Industry	Attractiveness			
	Yes	No	Don't Know	No Response
Manufacturing	61%	—	39%	—
Banking	73	—	27	—
Utilities	49	—	49	2%
Retailing	59	6%	29	6
Wholesaling	80	—	20	—
Service industries	58	5	37	—
Food products	73	—	27	—
Medical products	—	25	50	25
Transportation	60	—	40	—

Humor and Physical Attractiveness Linked

Is a sense of humor tied to perception of physical attractiveness? Not surprisingly, we found that these two factors tend to go together. Both are excellent indicators of someone who possesses a positive self-image. Table 3–11 compares the number of CEOs who report that others consider them humorous in relation to whether they think others find them attractive.

Table 3–11: Attractiveness Self-Perception and Humor

| | Do You Regard Yourself As: | | | |
Attractive	Humorous	Moderate	Humorless	No Response
Yes	63%	33%	4%	—
No	50	25	25	—
Don't know	52	40	7	1%
No response	100	—	—	—

Are Names Linked to Attractiveness Perception?

CEOs who use nicknames are the least likely to think others consider them attractive. As we saw in the birth order section of Chapter 1, use of a nickname is a firstborn or lastborn trait, and much less common for middle children. As Table 3–12 shows, those CEOs using a nickname scored substantially below average on attractiveness, while all other groups scored slightly above average.

One Final Classification

In looking for a relationship between attractiveness and college grades, we found an objective basis for the CEOs' generally positive image—those who did better in college are

Table 3–12: Attractiveness Self-Perception and Name Used

| | Attractiveness | | | |
Name Used	Yes	No	Don't Know	No Response
First name	64%	2%	32%	2%
Middle name	65	—	35	—
Nickname	56	1	43	—
Initials	67	—	33	—
Averages	61	2	36	1

more likely to believe others consider them attractive than are those who did less well. In particular, those who think others find them attractive were more likely to make either "As" or "Bs" than those who considered themselves unattractive, but those who have no opinion concerning their attractiveness were more likely than either group to make an "A" average in college.

Table 3–13 summarizes our findings on the likelihood of a CEO making a particular grade point average, given his feelings of attractiveness.

Table 3–13: Attractiveness Self-Perception and College Grades

| | Grades | | | | |
Attractive	C	B	A	Other	No Response
Yes	5%	56%	37%	1%	1%
No	25	25	25	—	25
Don't know	10	50	40	—	—
No response	—	67	33	—	—

Even though the "don't knows" were slightly more likely than the "attractives" to get an "A" average, they were also much more likely to get a "C" average, thus giving them both the overall average of 3.3 on a 4-point scale. The overall average for the "unattractives" was 3.0.

CEOs who consider themselves attractive did better in college, which may mean that they had more positive influences on their self-images than did our other CEOs. Because of this earlier success in life, they might have developed a positive self-image earlier, which is evident in other ways such as believing others find them physically attractive.

SUMMING UP

This chapter has given us a few more clues behind the reasons for the success of CEOs. The personal characteristics examined here are surely not the most important determinants of getting ahead in the business world, but there is little question that some of them play a role. For instance, there is considerable evidence that taller people are more likely to get a specific job, all other things equal. Our findings reveal that the CEOs of America's top corporations are considerably above average in height. Indeed, about 90 percent of them exceed the current national average, and an even greater proportion are taller than average for their age. One reason for this is that a large percentage of them grew up in upper class or upper-middle class families, and income has a strong positive effect on height, operating through the media of nutrition and access to health care.

Another factor that may contribute to the CEOs' successes is the self-perception of physical attractiveness. If they are indeed attractive, it is likely that this helped them to get ahead. In any event, the perception of being attractive is one element of self-confidence and a positive self-image, which certainly contributes to a person's success in any endeavor. We also found that those who consider themselves attractive did better in college than those who consider themselves unattractive, and better grades could be one basis for their positive self-images.

Since 1976, the median age of chief executives has increased by one year from 57 to 58. About 88 percent of all CEOs are 50 years of age or older. In addition, their median weight is between 181 and 190 pounds. There is a clear bias against overweight executives. Looking fit is apparently a prerequisite of success in business. Finally, CEOs of top corporations are even more likely to be right-handed than the national average of 88 to 91 percent.

Executives with aims as high as top management obviously cannot make themselves taller to get ahead in the corporate world, but the information presented in this chapter provides evidence of the need for added emphasis in other areas if they have to overcome a disadvantage with respect to personal characteristics.

1. Malcolm Forbes, *The Sayings of Chairman Malcolm* (New York: Harper & Row, 1978), 104.
2. Steve Baker, "Sick Jokes Can Be Healthy at Times," *Mobile Press-Register,* 19 May 1986, G1.
3. Norman R. Augustine, *Augustine's Law* (New York: Viking, 1986), 79.
4. Robert Byrne, *The Third, and Possibly the Best, 637 Best Things Anybody Ever Said* (New York: Atheneum, 1986), 161.

"The research by Professors Kurtz, Boone, and Fleenor shows that non-smoking is clearly becoming a prerequisite for rising to the top of the corporate world. This study is further evidence of the desirability of being a nonsmoker in today's business environment."

William Weis, Director
Smoking Policy Institute
Seattle University

4

PERSONAL HABITS

An executive's personal habits can affect his on-the-job performance. Any health-related habit, including how much sleep an executive gets and smoking and drinking habits, has an impact on how long he can stay with his company and continue to do a good job. Hicks Waldron, CEO of Avon, illustrates the point.

During one period in his career Waldron's unhealthy habits almost killed him, but fortunately only cost him his title as CEO of Heublein. Waldron describes this time as the most stressful period in his life. Within one year, he suffered the loss of his son and his first wife. His diet was overloaded with fatty food. He drank more than he should have, including a before-dinner cocktail, wine with dinner, and a nightcap. Not surprisingly, he landed in the hospital with pancreatitis, for which the only cure is diet and rest. Unable to perform his duties during months of recuperation, he had to resign as CEO of Heublein.

Waldron's story does have a happy ending. He regained not only his health but his title as CEO. His health habits changed dramatically; he now avoids caffeine, tobacco, hard liquor, and fatty foods.

SLEEPING HABITS OF AMERICA'S CEOs

Research conducted on the sleeping habits of CEOs by the New York executive recruiting firm Howard-Sloan Associates, Inc., revealed that 95 percent of CEOs from the 500 largest U.S. corporations slept at least six hours each night. In his study of 60 workaholic CEOs from *Fortune* 500 companies, William Theobald, a professor of recreation studies at Purdue University, indicated that most of his respondents slept only between five and six hours each night. By comparison, many health professionals recommend that the average male sleep eight hours nightly. (Seven hours is usually recommended for women.)

Still another study of 1,000 top executives (not all CEOs) by New York-based Accountemps reported that most executives went to bed before the late news (10:45 p.m.). Wake-up calls for these executives averaged 5:49 a.m.

Our results parallel those of the Howard-Sloan study. More than 92 percent of today's CEOs get six or more hours of sleep each night. Two-thirds of them sleep between six and eight hours each night; nearly 28 percent sleep eight or more hours; and close to 6 percent get only between four and five hours of sleep. What is most striking about these figures is the number of CEOs who sleep eight or more hours. This might result from the fact that we did not restrict ourselves to workaholic CEOs, and from the larger number of executives who participated in our study. It might also signal a health-conscious trend, with an increasing number of CEOs heeding the advice of health professionals.

The Findings Vary by Industry

Our data show considerable variation among industries as to the amount of sleep the CEOs get. Table 4–1 lists the percentages of CEOs in each industry with various sleep patterns.

Retailing and utilities have the highest proportion of CEOs who need little sleep each night; utilities also has a lower than

Table 4–1: Sleep Patterns and Industry Group

Industry	Number of Hours		
	4 to 6	6 to 8	8 or More
Manufacturing	4%	63%	33%
Banking	—	69	31
Utilities	12	64	24
Retailing	13	56	31
Wholesaling	—	80	20
Service industries	5	67	28
Food products	9	55	36
Medical products	—	100	—
Transportation	10	80	10

average percentage of CEOs who get eight or more hours nightly. At the other end of the spectrum is the food products industry, which has the highest percentage of top executives who get eight or more hours of sleep a night.

Are Sleep Patterns Linked to Social Class Background?

Is there any relationship between the social class backgrounds in which today's CEOs were brought up and the amount of sleep they now get? Since, for example, the utilities industry has higher percentages in relation to other industries of light sleepers and lower class backgrounds, one might think that the two are connected. Our analysis, summarized in Table 4–2, shows that this is indeed the case.

With the one exception of the majority of the lower-lower class background CEOs who sleep eight or more hours per night, the pattern is extremely clear. Those who were brought up in an upper class environment sleep more

Table 4–2: Hours Slept and Social Class

Social Class	Hours of Sleep		
	4 to 5	6 to 8	8 or more
Upper-upper	—	50%	50%
Lower-upper	—	37	63
Upper-middle	5%	67	28
Lower-middle	7	70	23
Upper-lower	6	73	21
Lower-lower	25	25	50

than those who were not. This is especially clear in the four-to-five hour category and, with the one exception noted, equally clear among the heavy sleepers. Since only four CEOs were brought up in a lower-lower class household, it is probable that this aberration has no significance.

CEO SMOKING HABITS[1]

Ever since the 1964 report of the Surgeon General of the United States, the link between smoking and a number of diseases has been generally acknowledged. Since that study was published, the number of smokers in the United States has steadily dwindled. But more than that, smoking has been stigmatized in American society. People who smoke are a minority—and an increasingly unpopular one. Smoking is banned in many public places. Ten states and about 150 municipalities have passed laws that limit smoking in the workplace.

In the general population, about 55 million people are currently smokers—35 million of them are men. This comprises 37 percent of the adult (17 or more years old) male population, as opposed to 52 percent 20 years ago. In the age groups most relevant to America's CEOs, 40 percent of males between 45 and 64 years old smoke, while 18 percent of men 65 or older presently smoke. Table 4-3 shows the breakdown for the adult population in 1980, as well as for males.

Table 4-3: Smoking Category Comparisons for Men and the General Population

Smoking Category	Men	General Population
Never smoked	35%	46%
Former smokers	27	21
Current smokers	37	33

The Cost of Smoking for Individuals

A Conference Board study shows that smoking is an expensive habit. It reports that the "average" household spends about $140 annually on tobacco. The amount of money spent on tobacco generally decreases as the educational level of the head of household increases. The figures range from a high of $190.18 for households headed by an adult who did not graduate from high school to a low of $77.15 for a head of household with a graduate degree.

The Cost of Smoking for Companies

Industry research by professor William Weis of Seattle University concluded that it costs a firm over $4,600 more per year to employ a smoker over a nonsmoker. This is because smokers suffer substantially greater rates of absenteeism, disability, industrial accidents, and working-age mortality, and because smoke in the workplace results in damage to sensitive equipment, especially microprocessor components, and office furnishings and fixtures. Routine cleaning and maintenance costs are higher where smoking is permitted. In addition, the annoyance and health hazard to co-workers imposes a substantial morale cost and potential liability cost on employers.

It should be noted that companies can legally discriminate against smokers in the workplace. Smoking, an achieved attribute like prior work experience or licensing credentials, can cause a potential worker to be systematically rejected from employment consideration.

Status and Smoking

The results of the Conference Board study have been substantiated by numerous other studies, particularly in regard to the relationship between smoking and social or occupational status. A study by Lirio S. Covey and Ernst L. Wynder found that "smoking was linked to one's occupational level." They reported that professionals had a much higher rate of never having smoked than any other occupational group, and that current smokers were less and less represented among job categories as they increased in occupational status. According to Covey and Wynder, "physicians, dentists, business executives and engineers" were among the job categories with above average levels of workers who had never smoked. In addition, more than half of the professionals who smoked previously had quit smoking. Professionals did, however, have a higher rate of smoking pipes and cigars.

Other experts concur that smoking is becoming an issue that pertains to lower class individuals. As John Pinney of Harvard bluntly puts it, "Smoking is slowly becoming a lower socioeconomic problem."[2] The Centers for Disease Control agree with the findings of the Conference Board survey in that rates of smoking decrease with increasing educational levels. Other studies confirm the connection between smoking and job status. Research by Alfred Marcus of UCLA's Cancer Center indicates that about half of all blue-collar workers smoke, but only about a quarter of professionals do.

Executive Smoking Patterns

As several of the previously mentioned studies have implied, business executives have lower rates of smoking than the national average. It may be, as Pinney suggests, that the affluent pay more attention to their longevity and think they can do something about it. If that is the case, we would expect lower frequencies of smoking in executive boardrooms.

Several studies have focused more closely on top executives. The Howard-Sloan study, mentioned in the sleep habits section, also surveyed participants on their smoking behavior. Of their CEO respondents, 84 percent were nonsmokers. Perhaps a third of this group used to smoke, but no longer do so. Similar results were reported in a University of Michigan survey of three executive groups: chairmen of the board, presidents, and vice presidents. Of the 818 respondents in this study, only 20 percent were smokers, one-third were ex-smokers, and 47 percent had never smoked.

In a study of vice presidents and personnel managers by the executive recruitment firm Robert Half International, 22 percent of the respondents said they were smokers. An astounding 61 percent reported they had given up the habit. What is especially significant about this study is that the respondents indicated that there were decreasing proportions of smokers as one went up the management ladder. Another Robert Half study suggested that managers tended to favor nonsmokers over smokers in hiring decisions by a staggering 15 to 1 ratio, when the two candidates were otherwise equally qualified. Thus, there is good reason to believe that smoking is becoming a hindrance to getting ahead in business.

The suggestion that smoking has become an executive career barrier is supported by people like Barbara Hackman Franklin, a board member at Westinghouse, Dow Chemical, Black & Decker, and Aetna Life & Casualty. She says that many corporations now have unwritten policies that ban smokers from future promotion. Still other executives have exposed their displeasure with smokers more directly. Ralston Purina chairman William Stiritz once blasted a cigar-smoking manager. The chairman's ire was quickly communicated throughout Ralston Purina.

How Current CEO Smoking Data Break Down by Industry

Our study found more smokers among the ranks of CEOs than did the Howard-Sloan study. In contrast to their statistic—16 percent smokers—we found that 23 percent of all CEOs are smokers. We did find substantial variation among industries, from a high of nearly 40 percent in banking to a low of none in wholesaling, as Table 4–4 shows. There is almost perfect symmetry: four industries are above the overall average, one is almost exactly at the average, and four are clearly below the average.

Table 4–4: Smoking Preference and Industry Groups

Industry	Smokers
Banking	38%
Retailing	29
Food products	27
Medical products	25
Service industries	22
Manufacturing	19
Utilities	12
Transportation	10
Wholesaling	—

Now Let's Look at Social Class Backgrounds

When CEOs' social class backgrounds were examined to see what influence that may have had on their smoking habits, the results were quite diverse. While CEOs from upper-upper class backgrounds have the highest levels of smoking, those from lower-lower class backgrounds have the lowest. In between, there is substantial variation, as Table 4–5 shows. However, because of the fall-rise pattern of responses, it is difficult to establish a connection between smoking and social class background.

Table 4–5: Social Class and Smoking Preference

Class	Smokers
Upper-upper	30%
Lower-upper	13
Upper-middle	25
Lower-middle	20
Upper-lower	26
Lower-lower	—

Nonsmoking Is Associated with a Healthy Lifestyle

To shed more light on the health-consciousness of today's CEOs, our data were analyzed to see if a relationship between smoking habits and exercise habits exists. Of those CEOs who regularly exercise, only about 18 percent are smokers. By contrast, of those who do not exercise, almost half smoke. CEOs who smoke are much less inclined to exercise. Those who do not exercise have a one in two probability of being a smoker, while only one in five exercisers smokes. It is clear that CEOs not only smoke considerably less than the national average for men (23 percent versus 37 percent), but that nonsmokers are also more likely to be health-conscious in terms of exercising.

Exercise buff John Teets, chairman of Greyhound Corporation, is a prime example. His daily exercise routine includes running three miles, working out for an hour on a weight machine, and climbing 19 flights of stairs to his office at work. Encouraging employees to follow suit, he offers prizes to fellow stair climbers. In 1986, Greyhound banned smoking in its offices, a move supported by its chief executive. Nonsmokers, Teets claims, "are more active and have fewer health problems."[3] The no-smoking policy is part of a companywide campaign to promote employee health. To help them kick the habit, Greyhound offers free workshops to employees who smoke.

CEOs AND ALCOHOL

About 80 percent of America's 125 million adults drink. It is no surprise that CEOs are drinkers as well. Most of the top executives—94 percent—in a University of Michigan study of corporate leaders reported being drinkers. Of those who drink, 60 percent can be considered light drinkers, having fewer than seven drinks a week. Twenty-nine percent drink between seven and 13 drinks per week; 10 percent have between 14 and 20 drinks; and only 1 percent has more than 21 drinks weekly.

One study concluded that scotch and wine are the alcoholic drinks most preferred by CEOs. This research also debunks the myth of the "three-martini lunch." It turns out that only 7 percent of the CEOs surveyed named a martini as their drink of choice.

A study by Canada-based Molson Breweries focused on chief executives' beer drinking habits. The survey revealed that over 75 percent of CEOs in top firms are beer drinkers. About 24 percent say they drink beer at lunch every day, and, of those with a bar in their office, 64 percent stock it with beer. The latter tend to keep imported beers in their office bars, although they generally drink domestic beer at home, according to the Molson study.

Only a few studies, however, have concentrated on the dimensions of executive drinking and whether it causes problems for the firms that they direct. A major concern about alcohol consumption is how it can affect an executive's performance on the job. Management professor Don R. Beeman has commented," . . . it is the light-to-moderate drinker who can present the greatest problem for your firm; their impaired intellectual ability is often not apparent."[4] Given the ubiquity of business-related and other social drinking, those who share Beeman's concern are still in the minority. More attention is focused on the top executive who is an alcoholic.

Researcher Charles Shirley examined the job histories of 25 alcoholics in managerial positions and concluded that most were promoted regularly. Their corporate climbs were not halted until the final stages of their disease. Some evidence suggests that top executives may be more concerned about their drinking habits than the national average. A study by the Opinion Research Corporation revealed that 18 percent of the executive respondents were worried about their drinking habits, as compared with about 7 percent of the general population with drinking problems.

SUMMING UP

CEOs seem to be a healthy bunch when measured in terms of their sleeping, smoking and drinking habits. Most get between six and eight hours of sleep nightly. Executives in retailing get the least sleep, while those in the food products industry get the most. We also find a very clear relationship between a CEO's family background and the amount of sleep he currently gets, with those from upper class families tending to get more sleep than those from middle class or lower class backgrounds.

The chief executive is also considerably less likely than the average male to smoke, with only about 23 percent of

CEOs smoking versus 37 percent of all American men. Other studies show that many executives are ex-smokers, and that there seems to be a continuing decline in the proportion of top executives who smoke.

Considerable variation on smoking behavior exists among industries, with bankers being the most likely to smoke (almost 40 percent), while none of the wholesaling CEOs do so. Interestingly, no real connection was found between a respondent's family background and his current smoking behavior. We did find that our numerically largest background, upper-middle class CEOs, tend to smoke slightly more than average for all CEOs.

While our study does not deal specifically with CEO drinking patterns, there is empirical evidence that they tend to mirror those of the general population. This may be one of the more worrisome personal habits for many corporate executives.

1. Part of this chapter is based on an article by the authors. See "Where There's Smoke, You May Be Fired: The Smoking Habits of American Chief Executive Officers," *Journal of Applied Business Research,* Spring 1988, 81–85. Used by permission.
2. Trish Hall, "Smoking of Cigarettes Seems to be Becoming a Lower-Class Habit," *The Wall Street Journal,* 25 June 1985, 1.
3. Dexter Hutchins, "The Drive to Kick Smoking at Work," *Fortune,* 15 September 1986, 43-53.
4. Don R. Beeman, "Is the Social Drinker Killing Your Company?" *Business Horizons,* January-February 1985, 54-58.

"I kissed my first girl and smoked my first cigarette on the same day. I haven't had time for tobacco since."

Arturo Toscanini[1]

5

MARRIAGE

Marriage is an important factor in the lives of corporate CEOs. Most of today's CEOs are devoted husbands and family men, agreeing with Louis Auchincloss that "only little boys and old men sneer at love."[2] Frank Lorenzo of Texas Air Corporation—the owner of Continental Airlines, Eastern Airlines, and New York Air—is a good example. Lorenzo's office is decorated with numerous photographs of his wife and their four children. Chrysler chairman Lee Iacocca gives the royalties from his best-selling autobiography to support research on diabetes, the disease that killed his first wife. Greyhound Corporation chairman John Teets preaches, "Your family is more important than your job."[3] He usually starts his workday early, before 7:00 a.m., and leaves the office by 3:30 p.m. He believes in getting home early, and expects his employees to follow suit.

Given the intense pressures of the modern corporate environment, it is surprising that the vast majority of today's CEOs are married, most to their first wives. But can an executive maintain a satisfying, positive marital life while simultaneously operating in the stratosphere of the corporate world? After all, as the saying goes, "If you chase two rabbits, both will escape." Before we look at the data on CEO marriages, let's consider the psychological factors inherent in the CEO's job, and how these factors can adversely affect a marriage.

WHO ARE THEY MARRIED TO . . . THE COMPANY OR THE WIFE?

According to Purdue University professor William Theobald, who is currently engaged in a 10-year study of workaholic CEOs, the family suffers as a result of a CEO's excessive devotion to work. Priorities of the workaholic CEO are: work first, family second, and leisure third. When chief executives do come home after a 60-hour-plus work-week, they are frequently drained of energy, and often miss important family events. They may also bring work along on what is supposed to be a vacation, and may keep in constant touch with the office for the duration. Not surprisingly, they are known to cut a vacation short to take care of something that comes up at work.

According to author Marilyn Machlowitz, workaholics often say they will change after meeting some important goal, such as becoming a partner in a law firm or landing a particular advertising account. She warns families of workaholics that they will never change because their work is their life.

Among the strategies recommended to spouses for dealing with workaholics are exposing the children to the CEO's work, and using his calendar with a vengeance to schedule luncheon dates and vacations. Ultimately, many spouses of workaholics must accept spending a lot of time by themselves and with their children. But this is not always the case. John W. McLean of Liberty National devotes considerable time to his family, and the results show. McLean comments, "My family experience as an adult has been completely rewarding in terms of the relative early achievements of my three children and the role I feel I was able to play in each case."[4]

Frequently, it is not his time spent at the office that causes problems for an executive's family. According to management professor Fernando Bartolome, problems often stem from the executive's inability to deal with family situations. While it is easy for him to see how much specialized training is needed to run a business, he thinks either that having a family is easy or that family rearing skills are learned by trial and error. In addition, Bartolome says, executives often make the error of not confronting problems as they arise, thinking they will go away or can be dealt with later.

The marital successes of our CEOs suggest that the interpersonal conflicts cited can be overcome. They have made the necessary accommodations, and there seems little doubt that the stability of their marriages helps create harmony between work and family. A strong family life "is the greatest kind of anchor in any kind of weather,"[5] claims John W. Ellis, president and CEO of Puget Sound Power & Light Company.

James R. Moffett, chairman and CEO of Freeport-McMoran, Inc., admits that he couldn't have accomplished half of what he has without the support of his family. Moffett gives 14 hours a day to his corporate work, plus serves on a long list of civic boards and commissions. His wife, Louise, is one of his biggest backers. "I'm here to take care of Jim Bob and the kids," she says. In spite of his hectic schedule, Moffett takes time to spend with his children. He says, "If I want to do something with my son or daughter, I put it on my calendar. I make time. I tell myself I just have to be there."[6]

CEO MARRIAGES[7]

An overwhelming majority—24 out of 25—of today's chief executive officers are married. Less than 2 percent are single, and just over 2 percent are either divorced or widowed.

Most have successful marriages, when measured by the length of their marriages. Almost 72 percent have been married at least 30 years, with the median length falling somewhere between 30 and 34 years. (Table 5-1).

How common are these statistics? One indication derived from them concerns the length of marriages ending in divorce. According to the National Center for Health

Table 5-1: Lengths of Marriages

Length of Marriage	Percentage	Cumulative Percentage
Less than 15 years	1%	1%
15 to 24 years	13	14
25 to 34 years	42	56
35 to 44 years	39	97
45 years or more	2	99
No response	1	100

Note: Totals may not add to 100 percent due to multiple and no responses.

Statistics, of the 1.2 million divorces reported in a recent year, divorce was most common after one to four years of marriage.

The relatively short duration of marriages that end in divorce is an increasingly common characteristic of modern-day life. As Gerry Kinger, former president of Seattle-based Red Robin Company, put it, "You can spend years tinkering with a partnership or marriage, trying to make it work; but you know in your stomach from the beginning whether it will work or not." A Swiss proverb is even more apt: Marriage is a covered dish.[8]

The median duration of the CEO marriages that ultimately ended in divorce was seven years. Thus, it is clear that today's CEOs have more stable marriages than the general population, certainly when measured in terms of length of the marriages.

When Did the CEOs Marry?

Given the longevity of their marriages, today's CEOs obviously wed when they were young. In fact, 90 percent of them married during their teens or 20s. Another 7 percent married for the first time during their 30s, while only a few tied the knot in later years. One percent married in their 40s, and less than 1 percent in their 50s. It is interesting to compare our findings to national statistics on the median age at first marriage for males. This figure has risen from a low of 23 in 1956 to 26 today.

Frank Shrontz of Boeing illustrates the tendency of the CEO to marry young. As a college junior, Shrontz spotted an attractive young woman, Harriet Houghton, on campus. Shrontz announced to his friends that he would marry this girl. He did; and Mr. and Mrs. Shrontz recently celebrated their 38th anniversary.

Number of Marriages

Despite the fact that most chief executive officers have been married quite a long time, not all of them are with their first wives. While the majority of today's CEOs are still married to their first wives, including such people as Sam Walton of Wal-Mart and An Wang of Wang Labs, top executives do run the gamut of marital history. Some are still single, such as Leslie Wexner of The Limited and Steven Rothmeier of NWA, Inc. Others, such as Edgar Bronfman of Seagram Company and Milton Petrie of Petrie Stores, have had multiple divorces.

In the general population, divorces are on the rise. Consequently, so are remarriages. While there are no available statistics on the number of second marriages, third marriages, and so on, data do exist on the total number of remarriages. For example, of the 1.8 million marriages in 1981, one-third represented remarriages. But remarriage is not all that common among CEOs. Most CEOs have been married once (84 percent), almost 14 percent have been married two times, and just over 2 percent are in a third marriage. Combining the percentage of CEOs who have had multiple marriages with those currently divorced or widowed gives us a maximum of 18 percent who have ever been divorced (since some of them have been widowed).

This corresponds closely to the finding of the executive search firm Heidrick & Struggles, which revealed that less than one in five CEOs had been divorced.

Similar results were obtained in a study of effective leaders in both public and private sectors, which included 60 CEOs, mostly from *Fortune* 500 corporations. Its author, Warren Bennis, the Joseph DeBell Professor of Management and Organization at the University of Southern California, concluded that " . . . all the CEOs were not only married to their first spouses, but also seemed enthusiastic about the institution of marriage."[9]

A stable marriage, typically the first marriage, is one of the most common characteristics present among CEOs. As comedian Woody Allen put it, "I'm very old-fashioned. I believe that people should marry for life, like pigeons and Catholics."[10]

The Social Link

A clear relationship exists between the number of times a CEO has been married and the social class in which he grew up. As Table 5-2 shows, the upper-upper class

---

Table 5-2: Number of Marriages and Social Class

Social Class	Number of Marriages		
	One	Two	Three
Upper-upper	60%	40%	—
Lower-upper	88	12	—
Upper-middle	84	12	4%
Lower-middle	82	16	2
Upper-lower	89	11	—
Lower-lower	100	—	—

---

background respondents have the highest proportion of remarriages, while those coming from the lower-lower class have the lowest. In between, there is little variation. An interesting fact gleaned from this data is that third marriages are exclusively a middle class phenomenon.

Marital Status by Industry

Some differences in marital status among CEOs are present on an industry basis. As Table 5–3 shows, the proportion of single CEOs is relatively high in the wholesaling industry. The food products, medical products, and transportation industries claim the highest percentages of married CEOs, while banking and retailing have the highest proportion of divorced chief executives. Equally clear, however, is that overall the variation falls within a relatively narrow band.

Table 5–3: Marital Status and Industry Groups

| | Marital Status | | |
	Married	Single	Divorced/ Widowed
Industry			
Manufacturing	96%	4%	—
Banking	94	—	6%
Utilities	95	—	5
Retailing	94	—	6
Wholesaling	80	20	—
Service industries	98	—	2
Food products	100	—	—
Medical products	100	—	—
Transportation	100	—	—

THE INFLUENCE OF PERSONALITY
VARIABLES ON CAREER SUCCESS

An executive's family and his relationships therein can have a major effect on job performance and job satisfaction. Joseph Rychlak has studied personality differences between individuals who devote more or less attention to their home lives.

He found that those who invested more time in their families and those who devoted a lot of time to their jobs had fairly similar personalities in regard to energy, tendency to dominate, optimism, and self-confidence. Interestingly enough, those more involved in their home lives scored higher on scales for leadership and autonomy, and were less likely to be authoritarian in their leadership styles than those who were more devoted to their jobs. In addition, the family-involved personalities were more likely to delegate responsibility rather than try to do everything themselves.

Rychlak also found considerable evidence, although not conclusive, that a manager's psychological well-being was influenced more by family life than by the working world. By contrast, those less committed on the marital-familial scale tended to be less energetic and more dependent than other managers, though they scored about the same on IQ tests and on their knowledge of current affairs.

However, it is evident in Rychlak's case histories that scoring high on marital-familial tests does not ensure success, nor does scoring low necessarily indicate failure.[11]

Rychlak cites several case histories of managers who scored high or low on marital-familial scales. One, a college-educated manager who strongly emphasized the priority of his family and his personal development over his job at the beginning of the study, had in fact done very well on the job, becoming a district supervisor by the end of the study. He was active in numerous community organizations; yet, at the same time, he spent a lot of time with his wife and children at night and on weekends, and frequently entertained relatives during the holidays.

By contrast, a college-educated manager who scored low on the marital-familial tests was characterized as follows. He was married to a woman six years older than himself when he came to AT&T. The couple bought a home and rental property together; and he did well on the job, reaching the district level toward the end of the study. However, the two had experienced problems when her mother stayed with them for several extended periods. As a result, they were spending less time together than at the beginning of their marriage. He blamed this on his job; but the interviewers were skeptical of this since his wife had gone back to college and he had joined a bowling league without her.

SUMMING UP

Successful executives value their marriages highly, and those who value their marriages tend to be successful in their careers. Almost every CEO is married; and the median length of their marriages is over 30 years, far above the national average. Indeed, nearly 72 percent have been married for more than 30 years. In addition, more than four out of every five CEOs married sometime during their 20s. Unmarried CEOs are most likely to be employed in the wholesaling sector. By contrast, divorced and widowed CEOs are concentrated in the banking and retailing fields. This information may have some value as a career planning aid for future CEOs. Coinciding with earlier studies, the vast majority of chief executives are still married to their first wives. The likelihood of a CEO having been married more than once is greatly influenced by the social background in which he grew up. Those from the upper-upper class are most likely to be in a second marriage, while all the lower-lower class respondents are still with their first wives. Third marriages are the exclusive province of the middle class.

1. Robert Byrne, *The 637 Best Things Anybody Ever Said* (New York: Fawcett Crest, 1982), 130.
2. "Thoughts," *Forbes,* 30 June 1986, 160.
3. Brian O'Reilly, "A Body Builder Lifts Greyhound," *Fortune,* 28 October 1985, 130.
4. Personal Correspondence, 10 October 1986.
5. Mike Heatherly, "John Ellis: He Holds the Power at Puget," *Journal-American,* 2 February 1986, E1.
6. Mike Sheridan, "James R. Moffett, Chairman & CEO, Freeport McMoRan, Inc.," *SKY,* July 1986, 40,42,46.
7. Some of the following material is based on a forthcoming article by the authors in the *International Journal of Management.* Used by permission.
8. W. H. Auden and Louis Kronenberger, eds., *The Viking Book of Aphorisms* (New York: Dorset Press, 1981), 192.
9. Warren Bennis, "Good Managers and Good Leaders," *Across the Board,* October 1984, 8.
10. Robert Byrne, *The Other 637 Best Things Anybody Ever Said* (New York: Atheneum, 1984), 101.
11. Joseph F. Rychlak, *Personality and Lifestyle of Young Male Managers* (New York: Academic Press, Inc., 1982).

"The most important things in life, I think, should be first God, then family, then work."

J. Peter Grace
CEO, W. R. Grace & Co.[1]

6

RELIGION

On the first Tuesday of each month, a small group of top executives from Boston begin the day with a prayer/breakfast meeting organized by Thomas Phillips, the born-again CEO of Raytheon. The agenda includes a brief talk on such topics as the economic rewards of moral introspection, and a discussion of spiritual and ethical questions. On a regular basis, Laurence A. Tisch of Loews and CBS studies the Talmud with a rabbi. Bill Marriott, chief executive of the Marriott hotel chain, is a deeply committed Mormon. He devotes up to 20 hours a week running the Washington, D.C., branch of the Church of Jesus Christ of Latter Day Saints. J. Peter Grace is president of a branch of the Knights of Malta, a lay Catholic order that supplies food and medicine to poor people worldwide.

Though perhaps not well-publicized, these examples are not isolated cases of the religious involvement of top executives. Whether they gather to pray and study scriptures, give generous donations to religious philanthropies, or devote time and talent to religious charities and causes, the spiritual commitment of many chief executive officers is strong. The Reverend Thomas Bowers of St. Bartholomew's Church in New York City says, "I see more people interested in the church than in a long time. Executives are coming in at 6:30 in the morning to study the Bible."

The fact that many of America's top corporate leaders are serious about their religion is confirmed in our study of

CEOs. Before we discuss that issue, let's turn to the denominational preferences of executives.

EARLIER STUDIES OF RELIGIOUS DENOMINATIONS OF TOP EXECUTIVES

A 1976 *Fortune* report on CEOs offered these generalizations about the traditional religious preferences of America's corporate leaders.

> For years, the stereotypical "right" man for high corporate office could be easily sketched in cartoon fashion . . . The most "right" religious affiliation was Episcopalian. For most of the century, Episcopalians populated executive suites wildly out of proportion to their numbers in society as a whole. As recently as 1950, for example, they accounted for almost a third of the top corporate officers—more than ten times their representation in society.[2]

The 1976 report then went on to catalogue a shift in the religious backgrounds of chief executive officers among the *Fortune* 500 corporations. Since the 1970s, these trends have continued, but the rate of change has been much slower. Other changes, too, have been occurring in the religious affiliations of chief executives.

Comparing Trends in Religious Preferences during the Twentieth Century

Data are available to examine top executives' religious beliefs over the first three-quarters of the twentieth century. Mabel Newcomer's pathbreaking work, *The Big Business Executive*, offers information about corporate presidents and CEOs which stretches back to 1900 and continues to as recently as 1950. In addition, *Fortune's* 1976 report on CEOs updates her 25-year-old data. Table 6–1 reveals the changes in religious preferences that have occurred since 1976, and compares the religious denominations of top executives with those of the general public.[3]

Table 6-1: Religious Denominations and National Statistics: 1900-1976[3]

Denomination	1900	1925	1950	1976	1976 General Population Percentages
Episcopalian	38%	34%	30%	21%	2%
Presbyterian	17	25	23	20	2
Methodist	12	8	10	9	7
Roman Catholic	7	11	9	14	22
Congregational	8	5	7	8	1
Baptist	2	5	6	3	14
Jewish	3	4	5	6	3
Lutheran	1	—	3	4	5
Unitarian	3	3	2	3	1
All other	9	5	6	3	10

Note: Totals may not add to 100 percent due to rounding.

The Newcomer data for 1900, 1925, and 1950 are drawn from published biographies of various executives. The lack of availability of information about religious preferences for many executives led her to conclude that " . . . there is a good deal of evidence that a large proportion of the executives do not belong to any church and have no strong denominational preference."[4]

Even recognizing the limitations inherent in her data, it is evident that the high percentages of executive Episcopalians and Presbyterians are significantly out of proportion to their representation in the general population. Together, executives from these two denominations accounted for more than half of all the executives in 1950, yet represented only one in 16 of the general population.

Why did Episcopalians and Presbyterians dominate the top corporate ranks between 1900 and 1950? According to Newcomer, many of the top executives in her survey came from families of British origin, and these were the families that occupied prestigious positions in this country at that time. The Anglican church, or the Church of England, became the Episcopal church in the United States. The Scottish Presbyterian denomination, the established church of Scotland, also took root in the United States. Newcomer reported that the Catholics among the executives were usually of Irish descent, coming from families which were generally not as well off financially. Thus, Catholic executives tended to cluster in industries such as railroads, where large numbers of Irish immigrants had been involved in construction and then worked their way up; and in utilities, where connections to the once powerful political machines were important.

Finally, Newcomer notes that 40 percent of the Jewish executives in her study had founded their firms, whereas— by way of comparison with another underrepresented group—only 7 percent of the Catholics had. None of the Jews were selected for a top spot in a company different from the one in which they worked their way up, while one-fifth of the Catholics were recruited directly from other firms for a top position.

The Fortune Study

In the years since 1950, a number of changes have taken place in the denominational preferences of chief executive officers. *Fortune* magazine's 1976 survey indicated that the overwhelming predominance of Episcopalians had come to an end. The big gainers are Roman Catholics (the percentage of Catholic CEOs rose by 55 percent between 1950 and 1976), Jews, and Lutherans.

RELIGIOUS DENOMINATIONS OF TODAY'S CEOs

We used an open-ended question to ask our survey participants their religious preference. What we found is that while Episcopalians are still the single largest group, it is by the slimmest margin ever. Moreover, they are not followed by Presbyterians, but by a group of executives who call themselves simply Protestants. After these come Presbyterians and, right behind them, Catholics. Table 6–2 shows the new breakdown of denominational preferences among America's CEOs.

Despite their relative declines, it is obvious that both Episcopalians and Presbyterians are still considerably over-represented among CEOs. Also highly overrepresented, though less noticeable since they are a smaller group, are the Congregationalists. The underrepresentation of Catholics and Baptists, by contrast, has declined, though Baptists remain dramatically underrepresented.

Table 6–2: Religious Denominations and Current National Statistics

Denomination	CEOs	Population
Episcopalian	17%	1%
Protestant	16	—
Presbyterian	16	1
Roman Catholic	15	22
Methodist	7	6
Jewish	6	2
Lutheran	5	4
Baptist	3	11
Congregational	3	< 1
Mormon	2	2
Other	8	—
No response	2	—

Note: Totals may not add to 100 percent due to rounding.

Religious Preference Is Correlated with Social Class

Several correlations exist between social class and the denominational preferences of our CEOs. Among upper-upper class respondents, for instance, the largest single group by far is the Episcopalians, accounting for 44 percent of the total. For CEOs from lower-upper class backgrounds, Episcopalians are matched by Jews with 25 percent each; while in the upper-middle class, Episcopalians (18 percent) are just nosed out by Presbyterians (19 percent).

This pattern of decreasing Episcopalian representation continues with each step down the social class ladder. The most common denomination for the three lowest classes is Catholic, with 21 percent each from lower-middle class and upper-lower class backgrounds, and a full 50 percent from the lower-lower class. Table 6–3 lists the percentages of chief executives of each denomination from the various classes.

Also worth noting are that Jews make up almost a quarter of the CEOs who came from upper class backgrounds, Mormons are concentrated in the upper-lower class, and Protestants are represented across the board except in the lower-lower class.

DEPTH OF RELIGIOUS FEELING

Our study breaks new ground by assessing the depth of the chief executive's religious feelings. Is he, for example, Catholic in name only; or does he take his religion very seriously? Two of our CEOs who do take their religion very seriously are J. W. McLean of Liberty National and C. R. Palmer of the Rowan Companies. McLean noted, " . . . I think my religion (Presbyterian) has had a very basic influence upon me since my childhood days. Indeed, it comes into play almost daily, sometimes in very subtle ways that I don't even realize until later." Similarly, Palmer commented, "I cannot know, but I believe I have been able to cope with disappointments because of my religious involvement—successes seem to be easier to deal with."

Table 6-3: Religious Denomination and Social Class

Denomination	Social Class					
	Upper-upper	Lower-upper	Upper-middle	Lower-middle	Upper-lower	Lower-lower
Episcopalian	45%	25%	18%	16%	6%	—
Presbyterian	—	13	19	16	9	—
Roman Catholic	22	13	11	21	21	50
Jewish	22	25	6	—	6	—
Methodist	—	13	7	3	9	25
Baptist	—	—	2	5	3	25
Mormon	—	—	1	—	6	—
Lutheran	—	—	3	11	6	—
Protestant	11	13	18	13	18	—
Congregational	—	—	3	5	—	—
Other Christian	—	—	2	3	6	—
Non-Christian	—	—	3	5	3	—
Other	—	—	5	3	—	—
No response	—	—	3	—	6	—

Note: Totals may not add to 100 percent due to rounding.

Background Information

One survey that deals with this question peripherally is a 1975 survey by Otto Lerbinger and Nathaniel H. Sperber, in which CEOs were asked whether they attended church. Of their 238 respondents, two-thirds categorized themselves as church-goers. In 1986, *Forbes* surveyed 100 corporate chiefs and asked them to state their religious preferences and how observant they were. Almost two-thirds of the respondents said they attended church or synagogue on a regular basis. Most claimed that religion was an important influence in their lives. Still another study—this one published by *The Wall Street Journal*—reported that only 14 percent of responding CEOs said they did not attend church at least once a year.

We set out to get a finer-grained reading of the CEOs' religious beliefs. It turns out, though, that even for the population as a whole, no clear measure exists for determining exactly what constitutes a religious person. In 1980, the

National Council of Churches labeled one-sixteenth of the American population as non-religious. At that time, just over 200 million Americans considered themselves religious, though only about 160 million were actually affiliated with a particular church. Some 36 million, or 16 percent, considered themselves nominal Christians.

Sixty-two percent of the U.S. population say they practice their faith. But according to a Gallup poll, the attendance figure for the overall U.S. population is only about 40 percent. Mormons and Catholics have the highest proportions of church attendance, with 53 percent and 51 percent, respectively. Jews have the lowest, with 22 percent. About one in three Episcopalians and Methodists say they attend church, while a larger proportion, about 40 percent each, of Baptists, Lutherans, Presbyterians, and Protestants say they attend.

Our Data Are Not Comparative

We asked the CEOs in our survey to rate themselves as "deeply religious," "somewhat religious," or "not religious." These categories do not compare directly with other studies that used church attendance as a measure of religious involvement. The most obvious problem is the question of whether those who attend church are deeply or somewhat religious. Most likely the number attending church includes most of the people in both categories. However, some people consider themselves deeply religious but do not attend church. Even more common are respondents who do not attend church but consider themselves somewhat religious. Still, we would expect a reasonably high correlation between church attendance and whether a person considers himself religious.

Our Findings

An overwhelming majority of the nation's CEOs consider themselves religious. Two-thirds say they are somewhat religious. One in six considers himself deeply religious, and about the same number say they are not religious.

The proportion of today's CEOs who do not consider themselves religious is less than the combined figure of non-religious (7 percent) and nominally Christian (16 percent) respondents in the National Council of Churches data. But because of the differences in categorization, it is difficult to make generalizations. If nominal Christians can be counted as nonreligious, then clearly top corporate executives tend to be somewhat more religious than the general population. If, on the other hand, nominal Christians are counted as somewhat religious, then CEOs tend to be less religious than average. However, both the Lerbinger/Sperber and *Forbes* surveys reported that two-thirds of chief executives attend church, far above the 40 percent of church-going Americans. Based on attendance, we may conclude that chief executives are more religious than the general population.

Why should this be? Several explanations are offered by Harvard Business School professor D. Quinn Mills. He points out that most chief executives are in their late 50s, 60s, and 70s, an observant generation. Business executives, Mills says, " . . . are comfortable with big institutions. I think they think religious participation is part of their leadership role. Most of them have stable marriages, friends and families in the community and feel that religion is an important part of that."

Is Religious Feeling Linked to Family Background?

Where did today's CEOs get their levels of religious feeling? To answer this question, we analyzed our data on depth of religious thought in terms of CEOs' social class backgrounds and number of parents while growing up.

A Comparison to Our Social Class Data

As far as social class background is concerned, we found that CEOs who grew up in upper class families are more likely to be nonreligious than those from middle class or lower class backgrounds. In fact, one-third of the upper-upper class background CEOs classified themselves as nonreligious, while none of the lower-lower class background business leaders did so. Table 6–4 shows the pattern that emerges.

Despite the fact that the upper-upper class background participants include the highest percentage of nonreligious CEOs, it is interesting to note that they also account for the third-highest proportion of deeply religious executives.

Table 6–4: Depth of Religious Feeling and Social Class

| | Depth of Religious Feeling | | | |
Class	Deeply Religious	Somewhat Religious	Not Religious	No Response
Upper-upper	22%	45%	33%	—
Lower-upper	—	75	25	—
Upper-middle	13	70	15	2%
Lower-middle	16	63	18	3
Upper-lower	24	61	15	—
Lower-lower	50	50	—	—

A Comparison to Our Parental Data

The role of the number of parents in the CEOs' backgrounds is somewhat surprising. We expected that people from two-parent families would be more likely to be religious than those growing up without both parents present. Surprisingly, exactly the opposite is the case, as Table 6–5 reveals.

Thus, not only are CEOs from two-parent households less likely to be deeply religious, they are much more likely to be nonreligious, compared to those from one-parent households.

Table 6–5: Depth of Religious Feeling and Parental Presence

| | Depth of Religious Feeling | | | |
Number of Parents	Deeply Religious	Somewhat Religious	Not Religious	No Response
One	19%	67%	5%	9%
Two	16	65	19	—

Differences by Industry

Our research shows that there is substantial variation by industry in the depth of the CEOs' religious faith. For example, the highest proportions of deeply religious chief executives are in the utilities and medical products industries, while the lowest percentage is in wholesaling.

Table 6–6: Depth of Religious Feeling and Industry

| | Depth of Religious Feeling | | | |
Industry	Deeply Religious	Somewhat Religious	Not Religious	No Response
Manufacturing	17%	64%	17%	2%
Banking	18	62	18	2
Utilities	23	64	10	3
Retailing	8	77	15	—
Wholesaling	—	100	—	—
Service industries	11	64	25	—
Food products	10	80	10	—
Medical products	25	75	—	—
Transportation	11	78	11	—

By contrast, the highest percentage of nonreligious executives is in the service industries, while the lowest is again in wholesaling (all of whom described themselves as somewhat religious) and medical products. Table 6–6 gives the details.

Depth of Religious Feeling and Marriage

One finding of interest is that depth of religious feeling has very little impact on the number of marriages the CEOs have had. As Table 6–7 indicates, all three categories are very close. Interestingly enough, if there is any trend, it is that the deeply religious are very slightly more likely to have had two marriages than either of the other groups, while the nonreligious are the most likely to have had three marriages.

Table 6–7: Depth of Religious Feeling and Number of Marriages

How Religious?	Number of Marriages		
	One	Two	Three
Deeply religious	82%	15%	3%
Somewhat religious	84	13	3
Not religious	81	14	5

RELIGION AND LEADERSHIP

Joseph Rychlak's study of AT&T managers included research on differences between religious and nonreligious executives in terms of their leadership capacities. Rychlak found that those more deeply involved with religion tended to prefer structured environments for their work and outside activities, and to take formal leadership roles within these structures. When not in top leadership positions themselves, the executives tended to defer to other top leaders. The religiously committed managers in the study were also more accepting of their own limitations, and better adjusted psychologically than the nonreligious managers.

By contrast, the nonreligious were more likely to be the hard-driving types who did better at getting promotions. But they also were more vulnerable to problems when they failed. For example, when Jerald H. Maxwell, the former chief of MedGeneral, was riding high on the wave of success, he not only spurned religion, he also discouraged his sons from spirituality. "I always told them that Christianity was for widows, cripples, and orphans, not for guys like us," he later told *The Wall Street Journal*.[5] But when Maxwell was replaced at MedGeneral, he became a born-again Christian.

According to Rychlak the less religious manager also tended to see authority in a different light. He was likely to feel that authority should be derived from the attributes of the person holding it rather than from a fixed structure. He felt more at ease in less structured situations, and did not need a set of rules to guide him. Rychlak also found that the managers who scored lower on the religio-humanistic scale tended to have more hostility.

Examples of religious influence on a CEO's leadership style are abundant. Sanford McDonnell of McDonnell-Douglas reports that he seeks general guidelines about business problems in his prayers. Max De Pree of office furnituremaker Herman Miller notes that he consults the Bible about leadership. DePree says: "The Book of Luke teaches me about leadership. James teaches me about the work ethic, and Paul about relationships."[6]

Our analysis of the data on depth of religious feeling shows that clear differences in the managerial styles of chief executives exist which can be related to their religious involvement. We looked at three aspects of managerial style: degree of organization, decision making approach, and sense of humor.

Religious CEOs Are Better Organized

The Arab proverb, "Trust in Allah, but tie your camel," appears to characterize most of America's leading CEOs. Our data show that the deeply religious are much more organized and orderly than those who are less religious. Indeed, the straightforwardness of the relationship is amazing. Note especially the first column and the last two columns of Table 6–8 to see the straight-line nature of this connection. Organization is measured on a scale from 1 to 5, with 1 being the most organized and 5 being the least.

Table 6–8: Depth of Religious Feeling and Degree of Organization

| How Religious? | Best Organized | | | | Worst Organized |
	1	2	3	4	5
Deeply religious	59%	36%	5%	—	—
Somewhat religious	42	39	13	5%	1%
Not religious	28	47	16	7	2
No response	33	67	—	—	—
Overall averages	42	40	12	4	2

Deeply Religious CEOs Lean Toward Consensus Decision Making

Kenneth Olsen, CEO of Digital Equipment Corporation, is a deeply religious man. Some say the key to his success as a computer entrepreneur lies not in electronics but in Christianity.

When it comes to making decisions, Olsen claims that "a good manager never has to make any decisions at all." By using committees, Olsen encourages consensus decision making. His approach involves subjecting managers to endless review sessions until the complexity of an issue wears away and the problem at hand gives way to a consensus solution. Olsen describes it this way: "If those responsible do thorough preparation, the necessary decision is almost always obvious—or else it becomes obvious with hour after hour of working over the details. The most important decision I make is when to break for lunch."

Olsen's consensus approach to decision making exemplifies one of our findings on the relationship between depth of religious feeling and managerial decision making. We asked our CEOs which decision making style they preferred: making decisions by themselves; making decisions in conjunction with others; or encouraging others to make decisions by consensus. Whether deeply religious, somewhat religious, or not religious, four out of five CEOs in each category favored making decisions in conjunction with others. But our data revealed the deeply religious CEOs, like Kenneth Olsen, are more likely to use consensus decision making than are their less religious colleagues—about three times more likely than the somewhat religious and about 50 percent more likely than the nonreligious.

Religious CEOs Are a Funny Lot

Our analysis of data regarding depth of religious feeling in terms of the CEOs' reports on how humorous their family and friends consider them revealed that the deeply religious are more humorous than those who are less religious.

This finding, along with the one regarding organization, tends to confirm Rychlak's report that the more deeply religious managers tend to be better adjusted psychologically than those who are less committed religiously. In particular, we found that those who are deeply religious were also more likely to report that their family and associates consider them very humorous. Similarly, we found that they are also less likely to be considered as having little humor (only one respondent said his family and friends would call him humorless). Table 6–9 uses a scale from 1 to 5 as a measure for humor, with 1 being very humorous and 5 being humorless.

Table 6–9: Depth of Religious Feeling and Degree of Humor

How Religious?	Very Humorous				Humorless
	1	2	3	4	5
Deeply religious	20%	33%	44%	3%	—
Somewhat religious	13	48	34	4	1%
Not religious	14	46	33	7	—
Overall averages	14	45	35	5	1

Fred Roach of Centennial Homes provides a good illustration of the humor of religious top executives. While heading another firm, Roach once fired a purchasing agent for violating the firm's conflict-of-interest policy. The man responded, "You can't do this. Jesus tells us to forgive 70 times 7." Roach shot back, "I'm not Jesus, and you're still fired."[7]

SUMMING UP

The picture we have drawn of the religious affiliations of chief executive officers shows substantial variation from that of the general population. The most dramatic difference is the overrepresentation of Episcopalians and, to a slightly lesser extent, Presbyterians in top corporate offices. This is no longer the whole story, however. As recently as 1950, these two denominations accounted for over half of all corporate presidents and chairmen in the country. In 1976, they still held 40 percent of the CEO slots. Today only about one-third of all chief executives are members of these two denominations.

The real story of the religion of CEOs in the twentieth century is the diffusion of top positions among members of different denominations. Concomitant with the decrease of

Episcopalians and Presbyterians is the increasing presence in the boardrooms of such previously underrepresented groups as Catholics, Jews, and Baptists. In addition, we are also witnessing a rise in the proportion of CEOs describing themselves simply as Protestant, and a rise in the number of Mormons in top spots in corporate America.

As we expected, we found a clear connection between denominational preference and the social class in which a respondent was reared. Episcopalians account for over 40 percent of all upper-upper class participants in this study, and Jews make up almost one-fourth of all upper class CEOs. By contrast, Catholics are heavily represented among the bottom three classes.

We also found that top American executives take their religion seriously. Over 80 percent of them describe themselves as at least somewhat religious, and other evidence suggests that the CEO is much more likely to attend church than is the average American.

Depth of religious belief is also clearly related to social background. A third of upper-upper class respondents and a fourth of lower-upper class respondents describe themselves as not religious. Between 15 and 20 percent of the middle class and upper-lower class so describe themselves, while none of the lower-lower class are nonreligious. Interestingly enough, CEOs who came from two-parent households are more likely to consider themselves not religious than those from one-parent households.

Industry differences are pronounced, with medical products and utilities having the most religious CEOs and service industries having the least religious CEOs. Depth of religious feeling had a negligible impact on the number of marriages the respondent reported. This finding is something of a surprise.

Finally, our findings tend to confirm Rychlak's view that more religiously committed managers are better adjusted psychologically than are their less religious peers. Our data analyses show that the more religious are clearly more organized, and are more likely to be considered humorous by their family and associates. Deeply religious CEOs tend to encourage decision making by consensus to a greater extent than do their less religious colleagues.

1. W. R. Grace & Co.'s *1985 Annual Report,* 24.
2. Charles G. Burck, "A Group Profile of the Fortune 500 Chief Executives," *Fortune,* May 1976.
3. Mabel Newcomer, *The Big Business Executive* (New York: Columbia University Press, 1955), 47–48, and Burck, 175.
4. Newcomer.
5. Laurence Ingrassia, "Executive's Crisis: Aftermath of a Failure: The Collapse of a Man, The Agony of a Family," *The Wall Street Journal,* 12 March 1982, 14.
6. Edward C. Baig, "Profiting with Help from Above," *Fortune,* 27 April 1987.
7. Ibid.

"Educated men are as much superior to uneducated men as the living are to the dead."

Aristotle[1]

7

EDUCATION

Education had a strong influence on Jack Welch's business career. The CEO of General Electric earned a doctorate in chemical engineering at the University of Illinois. Prior to his doctoral dissertation, Welch viewed himself as "just a ballplayer." But his dissertation on condensation in nuclear reactor systems convinced Welch of his own analytical abilities. He recalls, "You go down 27,000 blind alleys. It doesn't work, you start again. You feel there's no hope while you're asking those questions, pressing, probing, pushing. But you have to get it resolved; otherwise, you'd spend your whole life looking for the ultimate answer."[2]

CEOs HAVE DIVERSE ACADEMIC BACKGROUNDS

The educational backgrounds of today's chief executive officers are both interesting and diverse. At one extreme are executives like An Wang of Wang Labs, who earned a Ph.D. from Harvard in just three years, and Dublin-born Anthony J. F. O'Reilly of H. J. Heinz Company, who holds both a law degree and a doctorate in agricultural marketing. At the other extreme are CEOs with less impressive academic credentials. Tom Monaghan of Domino's Pizza nearly flunked high school, and was later dismissed from the seminary for misbehavior. The rest of Monaghan's education consisted of reading self-help books while serving in the Marines.

CEOs ARE WELL EDUCATED

It is not surprising to learn that CEOs are much better educated than the general population. Ninety-nine out of every 100 CEOs attended college, and 91 percent graduated. By comparison, only about one-third of the U.S. population has completed at least one year of college, and about half of this number actually graduated.

These statistics bear witness to a long-term trend toward better-educated CEOs. According to the Newcomer study, 39 percent of executives surveyed in 1900 had attended college. That figure jumped to 51 percent by 1925. By 1950, 76 percent had attended college, and about 63 percent had college degrees. A 1976 survey by *Fortune* magazine of *Fortune* 500 chief executives found that about 97 percent had attended college, with approximately 87 percent actually graduating. The growth in CEO college attendance and college degrees is really the tail-end of a trend that reaches back to at least 1900 and likely even further into the nation's history.

The largest group of today's CEOs majored in business. This finding approximates *Fortune* magazine's 1986 survey of CEOs, which reported that 33 percent held undergraduate business degrees. The next most popular undergraduate major in our survey was engineering, followed by liberal arts. Table 7–1 shows the breakdown of college majors.

It should be noted that the selection of a college major is sometimes made on other than a carefully considered basis. This is true even for future CEOs. Roger Enrico, the CEO of Pepsi-Cola, wanted to be an actor while growing up in Minnesota's Mesabi Iron Range; but he passed up a local college in Collegeville, Minnesota, when he won an unsolicited scholarship offer from a business school in Boston. Enrico recalls, "At the time, I had no idea what a business administration college was. But then, I didn't really care—it could have been a school devoted to astronomy. All I cared about was that it was more than 1,000 miles further into the great big world than Collegeville, Minnesota."[3]

Table 7-1: College Majors of America's CEOs

College Major	Percentage of CEOs
Business	44%
Engineering	24
Liberal arts	12
Science	7
Law	3
Journalism	2
Other/no response	9

The Emergence of the Advanced Degree

To understand the extent of their educational backgrounds, we must look at the graduate degrees earned by today's chief executives. In 1950, about 17 percent of the nation's chief executives had attended graduate school. By 1976, almost 60 percent of the chief executives had had some graduate school. Today, 47 percent have earned advanced degrees, with an MBA the most common, followed by a law degree (either J.D. or LL.B.). One attribute that James E. Burke of Johnson & Johnson, Frank T. Cary of IBM, and Henry B. Schacht of Cummins Engine Co. have in common with a growing number of CEOs is a Master's of Business Administration degree. Burke and Schacht earned their MBAs at Harvard, while Cary is a product of Stanford's graduate business school.

The large numbers of graduate-degreed CEOs stand in striking contrast to the general population of adults over 25 years of age, where less than one in 12 has had five or more years of post-secondary education. Moreover, of all degrees earned each year, only one in four are graduate degrees. If this proportion were constant for degree holders, we would find something in the range of 6 to 7 percent of the adult population holding graduate degrees (since about 19 percent have bachelor's degrees, and there is a 3 to 1 ratio of bachelor's to graduate degrees).

Interestingly, a chief executive officer was less likely to earn a graduate degree if he came from an upper class background. Six CEOs from this social class background have an advanced degree, but 10 do not. On the other hand, half the CEOs from upper-middle class backgrounds earned advanced degrees; one-third of those from the lower-middle class did so. Two in five chief executives from an upper-lower class background received an advanced degree. Finally, three of the four executives who identified themselves as coming from a lower-lower class background have an advanced degree. Overall, there is no clear connection between social class and whether the CEO earned an advanced degree.

Table 7–2 shows considerable variation among industries on the question of whether the CEO has an advanced degree. CEOs in the medical products, service, transportation, and utilities industries are the most likely to have earned advanced degrees, while manufacturing and, rather surprisingly, banking have the lowest number of advanced degree holders.

Some CEOs Did Not Go to College

Despite all this talk of degrees, it is worthwhile to remember that not all CEOs are college graduates. Some 9 percent of America's CEOs that we surveyed did not earn a college degree. A few are college dropouts, including William B. Hilton of the hotel chain, and William H. Millard, formerly of Computerland. Both, however, have been listed by *Forbes* as being among the 400 richest people in America, now or in the past. Companies as diverse as Goodyear and LTV are headed by non-degree holders. Most of these CEOs share a common trait—they've stayed with the same company a long time, usually 20 years or more. Non-degreed

Table 7–2: Advanced Degrees and Industry Groups

Industry	Percentage of CEOs with Graduate Degrees
Medical products	100%
Transportation	67
Service industries	56
Utilities	56
Food products	50
Retailing	46
Wholesaling	40
Banking	38
Manufacturing	34
Other	50

CEOs are most likely to be found in people-oriented industries such as retailing, insurance, and brokerage houses.

Though we may like to think of these non-degreed executives as contemporary Horatio Algers, it seems that their days are numbered. As recently as 1977, 12 percent of the *Fortune* 500 companies were headed by CEOs without a college degree. Today the number has dropped to one in 11, and indications are that non-degreed executives are a dying breed. A recent survey by management consultants Heidrick and Struggles of chairmen, presidents, and vice presidents reported that only about 4 percent were non-degreed. Since presidents and vice presidents are presumably the people who will rise to the CEO level, it seems clear that a college degree is a prerequisite for the aspiring executive.

THERE ARE FEW BLUEBLOODS AMONG AMERICA'S CEOs

Chief executives are, for the most part, not typical of the blueblood stereotype. This is apparent in reviewing information on their high school backgrounds. For example, the overwhelming majority—77 percent—of our respondents went to a public high school. By contrast, only about 20 percent went to a private school, and 3 percent attended both public and private high schools.

Social Class Plays a Role in the Choice of Public or Private Education

Whether a CEO went to a public or private high school is a direct function of his social background. Those from an upper class background, whether upper-upper or lower-upper class, were extremely likely to have gone to a private high school—78 percent for the former and 75 percent for the latter. But the proportions completely reverse as one descends the social ladder. Seventy-five percent of CEOs from upper-middle class backgrounds went to public schools, 20 percent to private schools, and 6 percent to both. Furthermore, the more modest the CEO's family background, the more likely he was to have attended public high school. Some 90 percent of lower-middle class CEOs did so, as did 94 percent from the upper-lower class and all of our lower-lower class chief executives. The data on high school attendance also give us confidence in the assessments of family background, since we clearly did not have a great number of respondents having been to private schools identifying their backgrounds as middle class or lower class.

Differences Exist Among Industries

The data on industries show an overall pattern similar to that on high school attendance in relation to the class backgrounds of the CEOs. Utilities, with 82 percent, and banking, with 80 percent, top the list on percentages of CEOs attending public high schools. Next comes manufacturing, 79 percent; followed by transportation, 78 percent; retailing, 77 percent; medical products, 75 percent; service industries, 72 percent; and food products, 70 percent. Wholesaling has the lowest proportion of public school attendees, with 60 percent.

Part-Time Jobs Characterize Future CEOs

C. R. Palmer of the Rowan Companies was given a small weekly allowance—25 cents at age 5—with the understanding that a portion of it went into a savings account. He started working part-time on a newspaper route at age 12, and continued part-time employment as a grocery clerk until graduation from college. Palmer's father required him to prepare a personal balance sheet and review it with him on a monthly basis.

Palmer's experience as a part-time employee was not unique among CEOs. The vast majority—79 percent—of CEOs worked while attending high school. As might be expected, those who went to public rather than private schools were more likely to have worked; 85 percent of those in public schools worked, while only half of those in private schools did. All who went to both public and private high schools worked while they were in high school.

There is little variation by industry on this question. Service industry CEOs were least likely to have worked in high school, with only 68 percent having done so. Medical products (100 percent), retailing (88 percent), and manufacturing (87 percent), had the highest proportions of chief executives who worked in high school. All other industries were within 5 percentage points of the 79 percent average.

An Opposing Viewpoint

While most of our CEOs worked at part-time jobs in high school, it is important to consider other viewpoints.

Psychologists Ellen Greenberger and Laurence Steinberg have published a book entitled *When Teenagers Work*. In it, they argue that high schoolers who work over 14 hours a week can be disadvantaged by the experience. Greenberger and Steinberg say that working teenagers suffer academically, develop poor attitudes toward work, and sometimes use their pay to buy alcohol and drugs. A similar conclusion concerning academic achievement was reached by the Massachusetts Department of Education.[4]

Not everyone agrees that opposing viewpoint. One mother wrote to Greenberger and Steinberg as follows: "My son learned more at Burger King than he ever did in high school."

EXTRACURRICULAR ACTIVITIES IN COLLEGE

The next educational dimension examined involves extracurricular activities in which CEOs took part while in college: particularly intercollegiate sports, and whether they started a business or a club while in college.

Numerous Jocks in the Group

Overall, our chief executives were a very athletic bunch, with more than one-third of them possessing the physical skills needed to make it on an intercollegiate sports team. A much higher percentage of private high school graduates played sports in college than did public school graduates. In fact, private schoolers were almost twice as likely to participate in sports, with 57 percent taking part as compared with 31 percent of public school graduates. Six of the seven CEOs who went to both public and private high schools played intercollegiate sports.

Early Signs of Entrepreneurship

Almost one in four CEOs exhibited early signs of initiative, leadership, and entrepreneurial acumen by starting either a business or a club during his college days. However, significant variation exists, depending upon both the type of college attended and college grades received.

Here the patterns are clear. Students of Ivy League and other private colleges were much more likely to start a business or club in college. For both Ivy League students and other private college students, 28 percent showed such enterprise. Of those attending public colleges and universities, only 17 percent started a club or business.

Extracurricular activities of this kind were no barrier to good grades in college. In fact, the better the student did in school, the more likely it was that he would start either a business or a club. To be exact, of the "A" students, 27 percent started a business or club; 21 percent of the "B" students did so; and only 12 percent of "C" students did.

The typical future chief executive was not likely to display much entrepreneurship while in college, though those who attended more prestigious universities and those who earned better grades were more likely to have done so. This finding should not surprise us, since the chief executive officers of the largest corporations today are not likely to have founded them (Ken Olsen of Digital Equipment and Fred Smith of Federal Express are prominent exceptions). As indicated by the *Fortune* survey cited earlier, most CEOs are professional managers; therefore, they have less need for a high degree of entrepreneurship. Our results on entrepreneurial activity during college bear out this assessment.

COLLEGIATE GRADES

Chief executive officers made good grades as students, as one might expect of a group going on to graduate and professional school. By their own reports, the CEOs in our survey broke down as follows: 38 percent were "A" students, 53 percent were "B" students, and 7 percent were "C" students.

Medical Products CEOs Earned the Highest Marks

Variation of grades among CEOs in different industries is marked. Table 7–3 shows that the proportion reporting an "A" average in college ranges from 100 percent for medical products CEOs to 18 percent for chief executives in retailing and food products.

Table 7–3: Future CEOs' Average College Grades and Industry Groups

Industry Group	Average Grades		
	A	B	C
Medical products	100%	—	—
Utilities	49	37%	14%
Manufacturing	44	50	6
Transportation	40	60	—
Service industries	39	56	5
Banking	33	58	9
Wholesaling	20	80	—
Retailing	18	70	12
Food products	18	82	—

Who Paid the Bills Made a Difference

We asked our survey participants about the extent of their parents' financial support during college, and more generally, how the CEOs financed their educations. Our concern here was with the relationship, if any, between how our CEOs financed college and how well they did in school. Cross-tabulating the results for these two sets of questions, we found that the chief executives who received full support from their parents during college did not do as well as those who had to finance part of their schooling themselves. Of those who received full parental support, only 33 percent earned an "A" average in college. Another 59 percent had "B" averages, and 8 percent earned "C" averages. By contrast, those chief executive officers who had to come up with part of the money through their own efforts did considerably better. A full 44 percent made "A" averages, 47 percent had "B" averages, and only 6 percent had "C" averages. The most likely reason for this is that having to put their own resources into their college educations improved their motivation and, as a result, their grades were better.

Among the future CEOs who had to pay the entire college bill, the percentages break down as follows: 41 percent paying their full costs made "A" averages, while 59 percent had "B" averages. For those not paying their full expenses, 38 percent had "A" averages, 52 percent had "Bs," and 8 percent had "Cs." We should note, though, that those CEOs who had to pay the full costs did not do as well as the group not fully supported by their parents (of which they are a subset). Because they are a subset of this larger group, it is clear that since their proportion of "A" students is lower than that of the group who did not receive full parental support (41 percent versus 44 percent), they are actually bringing down the overall proportion. In other words, future CEOs who paid some of their college expenses were more likely to have "A" averages than those who paid all their costs. It appears, then, that for our respondents there is a curvilinear relationship between the amount of college expenses paid by the future executives themselves and how well they did in school. Up to a point (which cannot be determined from our data), paying their own expenses made them more serious as students. If they did poorly, it was money out of their pockets; as a result, they did very well. Beyond that point, it is probable that the actual work to raise the necessary money took its toll in terms of exhaustion and time away from studying, thus eroding some of the gains which came from being more motivated to get good grades. On the other hand, those future CEOs who were paying all their expenses in college did not make below a "B" average, while some 6 percent of those in the larger group (not receiving full parental support) did have "C" averages.

Scholarships and Grades

We also looked at the relationship between receipt of college scholarships and grades. As would be expected, scholarship students did considerably better than nonscholarship students. Forty-five percent of scholarship students had an "A" average, 54 percent averaged "Bs," and only 1 percent had a "C" average. Of nonscholarship students, only 36 percent received "As," while 53 percent had "B" averages, and 9 percent got "Cs."

SELECTION OF A COLLEGE

In looking at the type of college future CEOs attended, we found that almost half (43 percent) went to public colleges, and about the same percentage (44 percent) attended Ivy League or other private undergraduate schools, or either went to a combination of public and private undergraduate schools or gave no response. Private school attendance breaks down to 12 percent of our respondents having attended an Ivy League school, and another 32 percent having gone to some other private college or university.

The College Attended Varies by Industry Group

We found substantial variation in the type of college attended among CEOs of different industries. As Table 7–4 indicates, medical products CEOs lead the percentage of those who attended private colleges (all non-Ivy League as it happens); utility company chief executives have the highest proportion of public college graduates; and wholesaling CEOs have the highest percentage of Ivy League graduates.

Table 7–4: Type of College Attended and Industry Groups

Industry	Ivy League College	Other Private College	Public College
Manufacturing	39%	9%	41%
Banking	35	11	46
Utilities	21	9	58
Retailing	35	18	29
Wholesaling	40	20	40
Service industries	37	15	32
Food products	27	18	46
Medical products	75	—	25
Transportation	40	—	40

Note: Either no response or multiple colleges attended accounts for totals not adding to 100 percent.

MORE ABOUT MAJOR FIELDS OF STUDY

Earlier in the chapter we touched briefly on the college majors that predominated among chief executive officers. Now let's turn to an industry-by-industry breakdown of the most common majors.

For the 47 CEOs in manufacturing, the most common college specializations were accounting or business, with 35 percent of the total. Right behind was engineering, with 28 percent, followed by science, with 18 percent. Liberal arts was next, with 11 percent.

Among the banking CEOs, a 64 percent majority have business or accounting degrees. Liberal arts, though second most common, trails far behind, with only 12 percent. Engineering accounts for 8 percent, science for 6 percent, and other degrees for 10 percent.

The utilities chief executives tended to major in engineering (49 percent), to an even greater extent than did the executives in manufacturing. Other common degrees are business, with 18 percent, and accounting, with 10 percent. The remainder is split among CEOs with a number of different majors, including the only CEO in our survey with a journalism degree.

Of the retailing CEOs, 39 percent majored in business. Law and liberal arts were next, with 15 percent each. Various other majors garnered less than 10 percent each.

Of the wholesaling executives, 60 percent earned business or accounting degrees. The remainder majored in liberal arts.

Among the chief executives in the service industries, business and accounting degrees again predominate, with 44 percent of the total. Engineering majors are highly represented here, making up 22 percent of the CEOs. Next come liberal arts majors, with 17 percent.

Of the food products CEOs, 50 percent have business or accounting degrees; another 20 percent majored in engineering. The other 30 percent chose a variety of other majors.

Two of the four medical products CEOs are liberal arts graduates, the highest proportion in the survey. Of the other two, one has a business degree and the other an engineering degree.

Finally, of the nine transportation executives, four have business degrees, two majored in engineering, and various other degrees are held by the remaining three CEOs. This is the only category in which there are no liberal arts graduates among the respondents.

A Word of Caution

Although business and engineering majors predominate overall, this is due in large part to the fact that individuals with such degrees are so numerous in the business world generally. The question of what degree gives the best chance of long-term success in business can only be answered by using information on the overall proportions of graduates with various types of degrees entering the world of business each year. A comparison of the percentage of each category that makes it to the top could then be made. One might even suggest that becoming a chief executive officer is too narrow a measure for "long-term success in the business world," in which case an even broader comparative study would be needed. However, even a narrower examination of what proportions of the various degree holders become CEOs is beyond the scope of this study.

FINANCING THEIR COLLEGE EDUCATIONS

Methods of college financing varied significantly for the CEOs in our survey. The typical chief executive officer, as mentioned previously, is not an aristocrat whose parents could afford to send him to college and pay all of his expenses. Though this was true for a plurality of today's CEOs, the margin is very slim indeed.

"Who paid for your college education?" we asked. The CEOs' answers show a preponderance of complete or partial parental college funding. These two groups comprise over 60 percent, as revealed in Table 7-5.

Industry Variations Are Evident

There is substantial variation among CEOs of different industries regarding who funded their educations. Chief executives in the food products industry have the highest percentage (73 percent) of parents who paid the full amount of their educations, while wholesaling CEOs have the lowest proportion, at 20 percent. Percentages for the other industry groups are: banking, 64 percent; service industries, 61 percent; transportation, 60 percent; retailing, 59 percent; medical products, 50 percent; manufacturing, 48 percent, and utilities, 40 percent.

Again, there is a large amount of variation in the percentage of CEOs of different industries who paid their

Table 7–5: Sources of Funding for Collegiate Education

Funding Source	Percentage Reporting this Response
Parents paid full amount	31%
Partly self-paid	30
Totally self-paid	10
Scholarship	16
Other	14

entire college expenses. The wholesaling industry tops this category, with 60 percent of its CEOs who paid their entire way. At the other extreme is the transportation industry, where only 10 percent paid their entire expenses. At various points in between these extremes come medical products CEOs, where 25 percent paid their full costs; food products, 18 percent; manufacturing, 17 percent; utilities, 16 percent; banking, 15 percent; service industries, 15 percent; and retailing, 12 percent.

Considering a category between full and no parental support, we asked CEOs whether they had paid part of their college expenses. Overall, just over half—52 percent—said they did so. Of utilities executives, the percentage paying part of their expenses was 63 percent (the highest percentage of "yes" responses); transportation, 60 percent; manufacturing, 59 percent; medical products, 50 percent; banking, 49 percent; food products, 46 percent; service industries, 44 percent; retailing, 41 percent; and wholesaling, 0 percent (remember, though, that 60 percent had paid all their expenses).

College scholarship recipients also vary widely by industry. Among manufacturing CEOs, 44 percent went to college on a scholarship, the highest proportion among the industry groups. The lowest proportion of scholarship recipients is in the transportation industry, with only 10 percent. In banking, 15 percent of the CEOs took a scholarship to college, as did 26 percent of the utilities executives. Wholesaling and retailing are close to manufacturing at the top, with 40 percent and 35 percent of their CEOs receiving scholarships, respectively. In the service industry, 29 percent received a scholarship, while 18 percent of food products CEOs and 25 percent of medical products CEOs did so.

Ivy Leaguers Received More Help From Their Parents

Substantial variation occurs in comparing methods of financing college educations among the types of schools attended. Essentially, those future CEOs who attended Ivy League schools were most likely to have had all expenses paid by their parents. Conversely, CEOs who went to public colleges were more likely to have contributed to the costs of their college educations. Table 7–6 gives the exact breakdown.

The expected pattern comes through clearly in the first three categories, where Ivy Leaguers had the highest proportion of financial support by parents and the lowest percentage of self-financing (either total or partial), with public

Table 7–6: Collegiate Funding and Type of School

Source of Funding	Type of College		
	Public	Ivy League	Other Private
Parents	44%	72%	53%
Partially self-paid	57	28	49
Totally self-paid	23	12	16
Scholarship	29	16	29

Note: Totals exceed 100 percent due to multiple responses.

college graduates at the other end of the spectrum, and non-Ivy League private schoolers in the middle. The scholarship result is perhaps surprising, as one might expect that individuals coming from more affluent social backgrounds, with concomitantly better access to superior educations before college, would do at least as well as other social groups in winning scholarships.

PARENTAL INFLUENCE ON A CEO's EDUCATION

One often neglected aspect of a chief executive's rise to the top is the influence of his parents. Through many different channels, some direct and some very subtle, an individual's parents can exercise a profound influence on the direction his career takes. In a 1985 study, *Forbes* recounts several examples of a father's influence and the varied ways in which it takes place. It should be noted that many CEOs, such as C. R. Palmer of the Rowan Companies, think that a mother's influence is often more important than a father's.

One amusing anecdote concerns Armand Hammer, the chairman of Occidental Petroleum. When he was growing up in the Bronx, he played hooky from school, incurring his father's wrath. His father's response was first to whip him, then send him to live with family friends in Meriden, Connecticut, when he was 10 years old. Five years later he was allowed to return, and he proved much more conscientious about his studies from then on.

A more prosaic example, but probably of greater importance because of its subtlety, concerns William F. Kieschnick of Atlantic Richfield. His father, a carpet cleaner, gave him increasingly more advanced chemistry sets as he got older, beginning before he hit his teens. The "hints" took hold, and Kieschnick's interest in chemistry grew steadily, culminating in a major in chemical engineering at Rice University.

Similarly, C. R. Palmer remembers how his father reinforced his natural mechanical and numerical skills, even at an early age. Palmer got his first chemistry set at age 9, and his first carpentry tool set at age 11. He was also encouraged to help with the maintenance of the family automobile at an early age. In fact, he could jack up a car and change a tire unassisted by age 10.

A strong indication of the strength of parental influence is that of sons following directly in their fathers' footsteps. For example, Safeway CEO Peter Magowan's father was formerly chairman of Safeway; though, interestingly enough, Peter joined the company without the elder Magowan's knowledge. Mobil Oil chief executive Rawleigh Warner, Jr.'s, father was the principal officer of Pure Oil. And Armand Hammer traced his father's footsteps in his education, receiving his M.D. from Columbia University. This kind of influence should not be overestimated, however. Concerning corporate founders, psychologist and ex-*Forbes* columnist Srully Blotnick found that only about once in 26 times would a child of the founder later succeed to the CEO spot.

EDUCATIONAL PORTRAITS BY INDUSTRY

Now let's tie together the information available on the educations of chief executive officers. To do this, we developed educational profiles of the "typical" CEO in each industry. Let's begin by noting several educational characteristics common to CEOs in all of the industries we surveyed. First, the typical chief executive is overwhelmingly likely to have gone to a public high school. Second, he held a job while he was in high school. Finally, while in college he did not exhibit an entrepreneurial bent by founding a club or business.

Manufacturing

The typical manufacturing CEO was a good student, earning at least a "B" average, and quite possibly an "A" average. He went to either a public college or to a non-Ivy

League private college. Most likely he majored in engineering or business. Costs for college were usually shared by
both the student and his parents. In addition, there was a
good chance that he received a scholarship. After earning
an undergraduate degree, he was not inclined to pursue an
advanced degree.

Banking

The typical banking CEO earned a "B" average in a public
college and, not surprisingly, did not go on to receive a
graduate degree. His undergraduate degree is in a business
field, though not in accounting. His education was paid by
his parents, and he was unlikely to have won a
scholarship.

Utilities

The typical utilities CEO made an "A" average in a public
college or university and later earned an advanced degree.
He majored in engineering. He paid part of his college
expenses, with the remainder coming from a variety of
other sources.

Retailing

The typical retailing CEO made a "B" average in a private,
non-Ivy League university or college. His bachelor's in a
business field is the highest degree he earned. His parents
were the source of his funding for college, though there was
a substantial chance that he also received a scholarship.

Wholesaling

The typical wholesaling CEO was in some ways the most
self-reliant in college. He paid all his expenses, and was
likely to have earned a scholarship in order to help do so.
He was the most likely of all CEOs to have gone to an Ivy
League school, though he was more likely to have gone to a

non-Ivy League private or public institution of higher learning. He earned only a "B" average (probably because of the time he spent earning his way through school), and he did not continue with his formal education after receiving his undergraduate·degree in liberal arts or business.

Service Industries

The typical service industries CEO also made "Bs" at a private college, but he went on to earn a higher degree. Unlike the wholesaling chief executive, he was subsidized by his parents in college, and had only about a 1 in 3 chance of having received a scholarship.

Food Products

The typical food products CEO was a "B" student at a public college. He was equally as likely to go on for an advanced degree as to stop after earning an undergraduate degree in business. For him, parental funding was the norm, and earning a scholarship was uncommon.

Medical Products

The typical medical products CEO studied liberal arts at a private college, got an "A" average, and went on to earn an advanced degree. He helped pay his way through school, but also received parental support.

Transportation

The typical transportation CEO made a "B" average at either a public or private university or college, where he majored in business. He then went on to earn an advanced degree. His education was paid for by himself and his parents. He did not receive a scholarship.

SUMMING UP

Having focused on the differences among CEOs of various industries, it is now time to sum up and look at similarities. Several important conclusions can be made.

First is the clear and continuing trend toward more education for chief executive officers. The CEO without a college degree is a vanishing breed; indeed, less than 1 percent have no college whatsoever. At the other end of the educational spectrum, there is an upswing in the proportion of CEOs with a graduate or professional degree.

Second, the overwhelming predominance of public high school attendees and the high percentage of respondents who attended state colleges confirms earlier research findings that corporate leadership is no longer the preserve of an aristocracy. This is also shown by the majority of CEOs who identified their backgrounds as upper-middle class. It is further emphasized by the fact that most future corporate leaders worked while they were in high school, and by the high percentage of those who provided part or all of their college expenses.

Finally, while business and engineering were by far the most common majors among chief executives, liberal arts degrees were still a popular option. Fully one-half of the medical products company CEOs hold liberal arts degrees.

1. Orginally quoted by Diogenes Laertius. Reprinted from *The Great Quotations* compiled by George Selden (Seacaucus, N.J.: Castle Books, a division of Book Sales, Inc., 1977), 68.
2. "The Man Who Brought GE to Life," *Fortune,* 5 January 1987, 76.
3. Roger Enrico, "Follow Me! The Path of a Leader," *Across the Board,* January 1987.
4. "The Latest Worry for Parents of Teens," *Fortune,* 2 February 1987, 10.

"People often play a sport the way they play life. Sports mimic business. You see the people who quit and those who don't."

Tony O'Reilly
CEO, H. J. Heinz[1]

8

EARLY SIGNS OF A BUSINESS CAREER

James R. Moffett, the CEO of Freeport-McMoRan, Inc., a New Orleans-based natural resources firm, played varsity football for the University of Texas Longhorns. Moffett remembers that his coaches selected a first team each and every day of practice. "They did that to remind the players that they could change the line-up if a player didn't produce. You were never sure you made the first team until you went into that locker room and walked up to that list to see your name. It reminded you that you had to work hard every day; that your performance wasn't based on what you did last year or last week, but what your are doing now."[2] This lesson stuck with Moffett, and he has carried it over to his position as a CEO. Today, he still asks his employees, "Do you want to be on the first string?"

A CAVEAT

Many top business executives cite the experiences they gained in school—whether on a playing field, in a classroom, or in an office—as crucial in the development of talents they used later in life. In this chapter, we will examine accumulated evidence from these early years that sheds light on what early signs today's CEOs gave of their future successes.[3]

Before we give the impression that it is possible to foretell who future chief executive officers will be based simply on signs that emerge during college, it should be noted that some business leaders are late bloomers. As pointed out earlier in the chapter on personal characteristics, the average age of the CEO has been increasing in the last 10 years. Five percent of the CEOs on the *Forbes* list of top companies reached that spot after they turned 60. Among them are John W. Culligan of American Home Products, who was named chief executive at age 64, and John Lynn of F. W. Woolworth Company, who became CEO at age 62. Then there are entrepreneurs like George Plumly of Plumly Industries, who at the age of 76 still works 12-hour days, six days a week. He started his first company when he was 53; Plumly Industries is his sixth company.

FINANCING COLLEGE

One clear sign of industriousness is working to pay for—or help pay for—college. Tony Burns of Ryder Systems, Inc., exemplified this trait while going to college. He pumped gas to pay for his undergraduate education at Brigham Young University. Then, while he was studying for his B.A. at the University of California at Berkeley, he owned a service station.

As we saw in the last chapter, four-fifths of all CEOs worked, and half of them paid at least part of their college expenses. These figures are considerably higher than estimates that 56 percent of current college students work while attending school. One-third of this estimated group work part-time and one-fifth work full-time.

Some CEOs financed their educations in unique ways. George Munroe of Phelps Dodge, for example, played professional basketball with the Boston Celtics and the now defunct St. Louis Bombers. He used his earnings to get a Harvard Law School education.

COLLEGE CONCENTRATION

One indication of a student's future business career is his major course of study in college. Some 44 percent of America's CEOs earned a business or accounting degree. Another early sign of a business career may be discerned in double majors; that is, graduating with two major areas of study. One CEO in seven was sufficiently industrious to take on two majors. The most popular choices for a second major were in the areas of law, business, engineering, and liberal arts.

INTERCOLLEGIATE ATHLETICS

Athletics are one of the most widely cited influences on an individual's career. Because there are so many athletes in the top echelons of business, the "dumb jock" stereotype appears highly inappropriate. IBM's John Akers was a hockey player, while Phillips Petroleum's C. J. Silas played varsity basketball. Alex Kroll of Young & Rubicam was an All-American in football, while Donald Rumsfeld (formerly of G. D. Searle), David Packard (Hewlett-Packard), and Paul Choquette (Gilbane Building Co.) were all varsity football players. H. J. Heinz CEO Tony O'Reilly was an Irish rugby star, playing for the Irish national team 29 times and the British Lions another 10 times.[4]

According to the National Collegiate Athletic Association, there are 268,000 varsity athletes in NCAA schools. This represents a mere 2 to 3 percent of the total student population in those colleges and universities. Among today's CEOs, 38 percent played intercollegiate sports. While a majority did not play, the proportion of those who did was overwhelmingly higher than the percentage of today's college students who play. Today's chief executive officer is at least 12 times as likely as today's college student to have played in intercollegiate sports.

Not only did these CEOs play in intercollegiate sports to a much greater degree than does the current college population, many of them played in a second, and even a third, sport. In fact, 12 percent (about four times the proportion of today's students who play any sport) took part in a second sport, and 2 percent were involved with a third.

Differences Exist Among Industries

The CEOs' participation in varsity sports varies widely among industries, with the figures ranging from a high of four of every five wholesaling and transportation CEOs to a low of none in medical products. Utilities and food products leaders also are considerably less likely to have played intercollegiate sports. CEOs in the other industries are close to the overall average.

SPORTS, GRADES, AND LEADERSHIP STYLE

Are CEOs who participated in intercollegiate athletics academic exceptions, such as Rhodes Scholar, former NBA player, and now U.S. Senator Bill Bradley; or does Alex Karras' description of his own academic career at the University of Iowa apply? The former Detroit Lion and sometimes actor once confided, "I never graduated. I was there for only two terms: Truman's and Eisenhower's."[5]

It is probably no surprise that those CEOs who devoted themselves to the athletic field paid for it in lower grades, at least in the aggregate. Since both those with good grades and those with athletic prowess made it to the executive suite, however, perhaps there is a trade-off at work here. In other words, one cannot say in the abstract whether the training of the classroom or that of the locker room is more important for later business success. In any case, the difference in grades for both athletes and nonathletes who eventually became CEOs is not huge, as Table 8-1 indicates.

As we can see, it works both ways—those who were athletes did not get as high grades as those who were not, and those who did better in school were less likely to participate in athletics. It is difficult to know which is the chicken and which

Table 8–1: Grade Averages of Athletes and Non-Athletes

Overall Average Grades	Athletes	Nonathletes	Average
A	35%	41%	38%
B	56	51	53
C	8	6	7

Note: Totals may not add to 100 percent due to rounding.

the egg, but calculating the grade-point average for each group provides an insignificant GPA difference of 3.4 on a 4-point scale for the nonathletes, and 3.3 for the athletes.

Athletes Are Less Autocratic CEOs

We found what may be the first empirical evidence that learning teamwork on the athletic field may have an effect on an executive's decision making style. CEOs who had been athletes in college are somewhat less likely to subscribe to the autocratic management style referred to as Theory X, and much more likely to use participative decision making, or the Theory Y approach. We must inject a discordant note, however. None of the CEOs who played intercollegiate sports subscribe to the Theory Z style of management, which is characterized by consensus decision making, while 6 percent of the nonathletes do so. Table 8–2 summarizes these findings.

Perhaps one explanation for this finding is that CEOs learned humility as well as teamwork on the athletic field. For example, Robert Mercer, the CEO of Goodyear Tire and Rubber, learned this lesson when he tried out for Yale's baseball team. Yale was coached by Red Rolph, a former New York Yankee third baseman. Mercer was trying out for third base also.

Table 8–2: Management Style and Participation in Sports

	Percentage of CEOs		
	Theory X	Theory Y	Theory Z
Athletes	9%	88%	—
Nonathletes	11	77	6%

Note: Totals may not add to 100 percent due to nonresponses and rounding.

Rolph insisted that Mercer move to an outfield position. He told the future CEO, "The way you play third, outfield's where most of the balls are going to go anyway."[6] Mercer obeyed his coach, and eventually earned three letters as an outfielder. He later tried out with the Brooklyn Dodgers,

Table 8-3: Sports in Which Today's CEOs Participated

	Percentage of CEOs		
Sport	Major Sport	Second Sport	Third Sport
Baseball	8%	—	—
Basketball	6	3%	—
Golf	2	0.4	—
Football	11	3	—
Hockey	0.4	0.4	—
Soccer	0.4	—	—
Tennis	2	3	—
Track/cross country	4	1	1%
Other	6	3	2

but did not stick. When Mercer went to Goodyear in 1947, he continued to play baseball with the firm's industrial team.

CEOs PLAYED MANY SPORTS

Although CEOs took part in a wide variety of sports during their college years, football was the most popular. In second place was baseball. Of the CEOs who played in two or even three sports, basketball, football, or tennis were most likely to be the second sport chosen. Table 8–3 shows the proportion of chief executives in each sport, and the number who played in the various sports as their second or third sport.

The Industry Connection

A relationship exists between sports played by the CEOs in college and the industries headed by the CEOs today. Some are clearly "football industries," while in others baseball or basketball predominates. Other sports preferences are scattered among a number of industries, without any meaningful concentration. Table 8–4 gives the details.

While football was the most popular collegiate sport overall, and the most popular in four particular industries, it has a big edge over the competition in only two of them. Baseball and basketball were by far the most popular sports among current CEOs in the two industries in which they are most common. One less popular sport should be noted: track/cross country was actually the second most common sport among present manufacturing CEOs, with 9 percent of that group.

CAMPUS ACTIVITIES

Sports competition is not the only way in which future chief executives can distinguish themselves during their college

Table 8–4: Sports Participation and Industry Groups

Industry	Percentage of CEOs			
	Baseball	Football	Basketball	Others
Manufacturing	7%	11%	7%	20%
Banking	7	9	2	16
Utilities	2	7	5	12
Retailing	6	6	18	6
Wholesaling	—	20	60	—
Service industries	10	20	2	15
Food products	18	9	—	—
Medical products	—	—	—	—
Transportation	30	20	10	20

Note: Totals may not add to 100 percent due to multiple responses and nonresponses.

careers. The importance of one campus activity—ROTC—has been highlighted in a series of recruiting advertisements that feature leading corporate executives, such as Sherwin-William's CEO John G. Breen, Mobil's Rawleigh Warner, Jr., and Walter F. Williams of Bethlehem Steel, who all began their careers as Army second lieutenants.

Extracurricular activities are likely to characterize the future business leader. In fact, mere participation in a campus organization is so common among CEOs that it does not tell us very much. What is more revealing is the number of future executives who held an office in a club, fraternity, or other organization during their college years. To be exact, almost three of every four CEOs held office in a group in which they were involved on campus.

Again ... the Industry Connection

Although most CEOs held an office in a club or other organization while they were in college, substantial variation exists among chief executives in different industries. Some interesting contrasts with the information on athletic participation can be seen. For example, the medical products CEOs, none of whom were athletes, all held an office in a campus organization. Similarly, the wholesalers, who had the highest proportion of college athletes, had the second-lowest rate of club officers of any industry. On the other hand, transportation executives, who are also at the top in sports participation, show a significantly above average rate of holding campus office. Table 8–5 shows the percentages of chief executives in each industry who held an office in a campus organization while they were in college.

We notice, too, that the utilities industry stands out once again. Just as it has one of the highest percentages of lower class background CEOs and public college graduates, it has the lowest rate of office holders in college. So, in yet another way, utilities chief executives turn out to be hard to distinguish from the mainstream population.

Table 8–5: Campus Club Officers and Industry Groups

Industry	Club Officers
Manufacturing	69%
Banking	84
Utilities	58
Retailing	71
Wholesaling	60
Service industries	66
Food products	64
Medical products	100
Transportation	80

No Social Class Pattern Exists

In analyzing the relationship between the office holding CEO and his social class background, we find that those CEOs who grew up in an upper class environment were less likely than average to have been a club officer. Upper-middle class CEOs were the most likely to have held office, while those from lower-middle class backgrounds were much less likely than average to have done so. Upper-lower class CEOs were the least likely to have held an office, but three-fourths of the lower-lower class CEOs held office. Table 8–6 summarizes these findings.

Table 8–6: Social Class and Club Offices Held in College

Social Class Background	Club Officer
Upper-upper	67%
Lower-upper	63
Upper-middle	79
Lower-middle	61
Upper-lower	59
Lower-lower	75

Overall, two-thirds of the upper class future CEOs held office, while 75 percent of the middle class respondents and 61 percent of the lower class survey participants did so.

Another Connection to Grades

In one respect, the influence on grades of holding an organizational office was similar to that of sports participation. In both cases, an inverse relationship exists between a respondent taking part in the activity and his grades. Some

71 percent of the CEOs who were "A" students held an office; 70 percent of the "B" students did; and 77 percent of the "C" students did. The trade-off, then, does not seem to have been very great, as "A" and "B" students held offices in almost equal proportions, and equal percentages of the office holders and non-office holders made "A" averages.

Type of College Attended Makes a Difference

Finally, we searched for a connection between the kind of school a respondent attended and the likelihood that he held an office in a campus organization. Interestingly, the highest proportion of office holders (81 percent) came from private, but non-Ivy League, colleges and universities. At Ivy League schools, the comparable figure was 68 percent, while still fewer public university graduates (66 percent) had held a club or organizational office.

EARLY ENTREPRENEURIAL ACTIVITY AMONG OUR CEOs

Many management theorists would argue that a sure sign of future business success is whether an individual started a business or club while in high school or college. This would be an early sign of the entrepreneurial spirit, surely a plus in running a major firm. Or so many people think.

In fact, of course, most CEOs did not found the firm they head, and the elusive blend of managerial talent needed to run one of America's top companies is not the same thing as entrepreneurship. Only 23 percent of the CEOs in our survey started a business or club while they were in college. This means, though, that almost one in every four future leaders of a corporate giant demonstrated Walt Disney's belief through early actions: "If you can dream it, you can do it."

Social Class Does Not Make a Difference

Interestingly, for the most part, entrepreneurship was not a function of the social class in which the CEO was reared. Aside from the upper-upper class, of which only 10 percent started a business or club in college, about 20 to 25 percent of each social class had started such an enterprise.

Industry Does Make a Difference

Substantially more variation exists by industry. That the highest proportion of CEOs who started an organization or business in college is found among service industry executives is not surprising, since entrepreneurship is probably more important there than in some other industries. However, in retailing, where one would expect entrepreneurial qualities to be important, none of the CEOs started a business or club while they were in college. Furthermore, the

Table 8–7: Starting a Business or Club in College and Industry Groups

Industry	Percentage of CEOs
Service industries	29%
Utilities	28
Manufacturing	24
Banking	24
Transportation	20
Wholesaling	20
Food products	9
Retailing	—
Medical products	—

second-highest percentage of executives who exhibited this sign of entrepreneurship in college comes in the utilities field, hardly a fertile area for new ventures. Table 8–7 shows the percentage of CEOs in each industry who started a club or business in college.

Type of College Attended Makes a Difference

A relationship exists between the type of school a respondent attended and the likelihood that he had founded a club or business. As pointed out in Chapter 7, students who attended private colleges, both Ivy League and non-Ivy League, were much more likely to have started a business or club than were public college students. Only about one in six of the latter did so, while a little over one-fourth of private college CEOs started such an enterprise.

Personal Characteristics of the Entrepreneurs

What type of student was likely to have started a business or club in college? Our analysis of two key dimensions—creativity, and verbal versus numerical ability—produced a clearer picture of the personal characteristics of these budding entrepreneurs.

The Creativity Link

Our creativity scale ran from 1 (most creative) to 5 (least creative). Table 8–8 shows the likelihood of CEOs at each creativity level having started a club.

The responses show that the more creative CEOs are considerably more likely to have started a business or a club during their college years. As another way of looking at it, CEOs in the top two creativity classifications comprise two-thirds of the business/club founders, even though they account for only one-half of all chief executives. Viewed from still another angle, the increased likelihood of the creative to be founders is evident.

Table 8-8: Early Entrepreneurial Activity and Creativity

Creativity Score	Percentage Who Were Founders
1 (most creative)	29%
2	28
3	19
4	6
5 (least creative)	—
Sample average	23

The Numerical/Verbal Link

Equally striking is the disparity between the numerical types and verbal types regarding the likelihood of their having started an enterprise in college. In fact, the CEOs stronger in verbal ability were twice as likely as their numerical brethren to start a business or a club. Interestingly, those who said they were equal on both abilities were just as likely as the "verbals" to have started an organization. Table 8-9 summarizes these results.

Again, if we look at the data from another angle, we find that the "verbals" comprise two-thirds of the founders, although they make up only 56 percent of our respondents. By contrast, the "numericals," who are one-third of all CEOs, comprise only 20 percent of the founders. "Equals" comprise 11 percent of CEOs, and give us 13 percent of the club/business founders.

SUMMING UP

The chief executives are a varied bunch, but one thing the vast majority have in common is that they gave an early

Table 8–9: Starting a Business or Club and Verbal/Numerical Abilities

Numerical or Verbal Abilities	Probability of Starting a Business or Club
Numerical	14%
Verbal	27
Equal	27
Sample average	23

indication of future success. In most cases, this was not an entrepreneurial bent, but another leadership trait shown during college. They also tended to care enough about their educations to work to support themselves in college, with about 80 percent working full- or part-time while in college. This compares with a figure of 56 percent of today's working college students.

A major distinction between the CEO and the average college student today is that the CEO is much more likely to have taken part in intercollegiate athletics. While only about 2 percent of students are involved in college sports today, about three-eighths of all CEOs were involved. Moreover, at least one in eight took part in a second sport, and 2 percent played a third. The transportation and wholesaling industries have the highest proportion of CEOs who were college athletes. By contrast, none of the medical products CEOs played intercollegiate sports.

We found, too, that the time spent on sports had little effect on the CEOs' college grades. Thirty-five percent of the student-athletes had an "A" average, compared with 41 percent of the nonathletes. Time spent on the playing field was not wasted either. Many CEOs who were college athletes feel that playing sports helped them learn teamwork and leadership, and our data help support this claim. The CEO athletes are less likely than the nonathletes to be autocratic, Theory X managers and much more likely to use Theory Y participative decision making skills.

Perhaps the most telling statistic on leadership in college is that 70 percent of the CEOs held an office in a club or other organization while they were in college. The wholesaling industry, with many collegiate athletes, had a relatively low 60 percent who were club officers, though utilities had even fewer officers (58 percent). On the other hand, the transportation industry had lots of athletes and lots of officers (80 percent). The nonathletic office holding future CEO experienced a slight retarding effect on his college grades, but smaller than that experienced by the athletic office holder.

Finally, we found that entrepreneurial activity—starting a business or a club in college—was not all that common among our respondents. Only 23 percent had done so. This was true regardless of social class (except that it was much less common among upper-upper class CEOs). The proportion of entrepreneurs varied from none in medical products and retailing to 29 percent in service industries. The student more likely to have started a club or business was more likely to have rated himself high on the scale of creativity, and to have rated himself better in verbal than numerical ability.

---

1. John A. Byrne, "Executive Sweat," *Forbes,* 15 May 1985.
2. Mike Sheridan, "James R. Moffett: Chairman and CEO, Freeport-McMoRan, Inc.," *SKY,* July 1986, 42.
3. Some of the following material is based on a forthcoming article by author in *Business Horizons.* Used with permission.
4. Thomas R. Horton, *What Works for Me* (New York: Random House, 1986), 339–40.
5. Norman R. Augustine, *Augustine's Law* (New York: Viking, 1986), 74.
6. Byrne, 199.

"I have outside interests and try to make sure that I don't think about the company every waking moment. I don't think that is healthy for me or the company."

Frank Shrontz
CEO, The Boeing Company[1]

9

LEISURE INTERESTS

CBS chief executive officer Larry Tisch offers a different perspective from that of Frank Shrontz. As Tisch puts it, "I find business very relaxing. I look forward every day to going to the office."[2] Although most executives would echo the CBS leader's sentiments on most mornings, not all corporate chiefs are workaholics. Most, it's true, put in long hours on the job; yet many try to strike a balance between work and leisure. Some, like Paul Oreffice, president of Dow Chemical Company, actually denounce the workaholic ethic. "I believe you have to lead a balanced life," Oreffice says. "I preach this to our young people all the time. If they become workaholics and their family life breaks up, they are not a success."

Oreffice, a devoted family man, lives according to his advice. On weekends and during vacations, he indulges his passion for tennis. "When I'm on the tennis court," he quips, "I forget what company I work for." He seldom goes to the office on weekends, though he does bring paperwork home. Vacations, for Oreffice, are times to break away from corporate responsibilities. "I trust my managers here," he says. "When I go on vacation, I will spend a whole week without hearing from anybody. It doesn't make me nervous at all. I'll never call them; they have to call me, unless something very unusual happens or is on. I can go away for two weeks and talk to the office maybe once or twice."[3]

CEOs' LEISURE TIME IS DIMINISHING

Long working hours are part of the job description for most chief executives. A 1986 *Fortune* survey found that the typical CEO works 59 hours a week, considerably more than the 55 hours reported a decade earlier. Almost half of today's CEOs work between 55 and 64 hours a week, and about one-third put in 65 hours or more. Three in 10 enjoy a shorter work week of 45 to 54 hours, and only a tiny percentage (3 percent) work 44 hours or less. As the poet Robert Frost pointed out, "By working faithfully eight hours a day, you may eventually get to be boss and work 12 hours a day."[4]

LEISURE—
A CONTROVERSIAL ISSUE IN CEO CIRCLES[5]

Given that most CEOs spend long hours on the job, leisure time emerges as a critical issue. Certainly leisure is something every CEO thinks about, if only to dismiss the possibility of taking time away from work. Others may require leisure to function effectively in their high-pressure jobs. How CEOs view leisure time boils down to two perspectives. There are those who take little of it and desire none of it. Mesa Petroleum's T. Boone Pickens, Jr. claims, "Work is relaxation to me. I have to keep busy just to stay awake."[6] Others, like Frank Shrontz, are convinced that taking time away from the job at regular intervals improves their overall job performance.

The Theobald Study

Purdue University professor William Theobald has encountered many chief executive officers who view leisure time as a waste of time. Currently in the midst of a 10-year study of 60 workaholic CEOs, Theobald has come to the conclusion that the work-driven CEO thrives on pressure and is excited and challenged by it. Ironically, these executives view vacation time as stressful. "So far I've found that most high-level executives prefer the boardroom to the Bahamas," said Theobald. "They don't really enjoy leisure time; they feel their work is their leisure. Most view leisure time as unproductive."[7]

When forced to take a vacation by a physician concerned about their health or a spouse concerned about their marriage, many CEOs suffer through it, preoccupied by thoughts of work left behind and by the actual work they bring with them in their briefcases. Those who feel particularly uncomfortable call the office several times a day to check in. "I can't help comparing these executives' descriptions of vacations with other people's descriptions of a stressful week in the office," continued Theobald. "The CEOs returned feeling irritable, fatigued, and with the same symptoms others report from overwork."[8]

The Arguments for Leisure Activities

Despite the feelings of the workaholic CEOs, most chief executives do manage to get away from their work. Almost one-third of America's CEOs take four weeks of vacation a year, and about the same proportion take three weeks. One in 10 takes five weeks. Those who get away for only two weeks account for one-sixth of all CEOs, and a still smaller proportion—about 13 percent—take less than two weeks.

Executives committed to taking time away from work often do so because of job pressures. Richard E. Snyder, chief executive officer of Simon & Schuster, acknowledges that he is a workaholic, but realizes that he needs "time off to clear my head." Says Snyder, "The pressures in business today are too extraordinary for people to perform an effective role all the time . . . I've learned to respect leisure time, and I'm encouraging my staff to take time off."[9]

Mary Kay Ash of Mary Kay Cosmetics would agree with Snyder's remarks. She says, "I like to work long hours, but if you have to lose your husband or family in the process, you're doing things the wrong way. It's no fun to count your money by yourself."[10]

Malcolm Forbes, head of the *Forbes* magazine publishing empire, believes that a chief executive who cannot take time off should not be in a leadership position. "Any businessman who says he can't get away from his desk is foolish and also inadequate. It's a reflection on his executive ability. The principal job of the chief executive is to have people who are probably better than he is at every single aspect of his corporation's work; somebody who is a crackerjack in marketing; somebody who can really give him counsel on acquisitions; somebody who's up to designing a good factory. The guy who says he can't leave his desk shouldn't be at it."[11] Roger Smith of General Motors offers a similar viewpoint. "Hard work is the only way I know to get anywhere in the world. But the work must be well directed and effective. Long hours, by themselves, are not productive."[12]

For some CEOs, vacation time becomes palatable only when leisure activities are viewed as a challenge. The same chief executive who is unwilling to spend two weeks lying in the sun might welcome the opportunity to spend eight hours a day learning the skills of sailing or tennis or golf. Activity and accomplishment drive the CEO, whether he is behind his desk or away from it. A spouse who understands this may orchestrate vacation activities that leave the CEO exhausted but satisfied. For many, this is the only kind of vacation that allows them to leave their work concerns behind.

Seventy-three-year-old J. Peter Grace of W. R. Grace & Company illustrates this phenomenon. Grace's leisure time is taken up with 12 civic organizations (of which he is president of seven), 10 club memberships, a bi-weekly business commentary televised on PBS, and homes in three states. He also serves on nine corporate boards and chaired a President's Commission on government waste. It is little wonder that Grace shaves in the morning while seated on his toilet. With all his responsibilities, he has to save time wherever possible.

For most chief executive officers, leisure is defined not only in terms of vacation time, but also in terms of everyday interests that transport them away from the pressures of work.

Many engage in recreational sports with the same vigor with which they engage in boardroom combat. Others paint, play musical instruments, photograph nature and family, or escape into the world of classical literature. Thomas Begel, chairman of Pullman-Peabody Company, unwinds by trimming apple trees and mending fences at his New Jersey farmhouse. John Emery, chairman of Emery Air Freight corporation, goes lobstering on Long Island Sound.

CEOs—who seem to connect every aspect of their lives with their work—often reap enormous benefits at work from what they do in their spare time. James Benham, chairman and chief executive officer of Benham Capital Management Group and trumpeter with the Full Faith and Credit Band, takes the connection one step further and sees his music as an essential outlet for stress. "I firmly believe I am a better manager because of music. For me, it provides an outlet for stress, similar to meditation. I can express myself emotionally, something that is rarely appropriate in the business world. It allows me to develop a side that could easily be overwhelmed by the pressures of the business I am in."[13]

In a survey of CEOs, the executive search firm Heidrick and Struggles reported that seven out of 10 chief executives believe that they do not devote enough time to their outside interests. The importance of these activities to the executive's business life is unmistakable. Whether a CEO consciously engages in a leisure activity to reduce stress, or whether he does it simply because he likes it, it is an outlet that for many is essential for effective functioning. For this reason, we investigated the leisure activities of the chief executive officers in our survey. Let's take a closer look at some specific leisure activities, including reading for enjoyment, engaging in exercise, and listening to music.

THE READING HABITS OF
CHIEF EXECUTIVE OFFICERS

Most people read for pleasure. According to the Book Industry Study Group, nearly nine out of 10 Americans who

read do so as a leisure activity. The group also found that
the average adult reads 10.8 hours per week for pleasure.
These reading materials include books, magazines, and
newspapers.

How do today's chief executive officers stack up against
these national averages? Almost all of them read at one
time or another for enjoyment. Over two-thirds say they
read frequently for pleasure. Less than 1 percent report that
reading for pleasure is something they never do. Of course,
what one person considers pleasure reading could be a
chore to another. For example, John Reed of Citicorp
relaxes with scientific journals.

Other Findings About CEOs' Reading Habits

Those CEOs who classify themselves as frequent readers
report significantly higher verbal ability than occasional
readers or those who never read for pleasure. While about
60 percent of frequent readers see their verbal ability as
their greatest strength, 51 percent of occasional readers
make this claim. Not unexpectedly, every CEO who states
he never reads for pleasure claims that his mathematical
abilities are much stronger than his verbal ones.

Reading patterns vary according to the type of high
school and college the chief executive officer attended.
While three-fourths of those who attended private high
schools describe themselves as frequent readers, only 64
percent of those who attended public high schools fit into
this group. CEOs are also more likely to read for enjoyment
if they attended an Ivy League or private college. Four out
of five in this group describe themselves as frequent readers, while two out of three who attended a public university
put themselves in this group. No matter the college or university attended, the higher the grade point average, the
more likely a CEO is to enjoy reading on a regular basis.
Nearly 70 percent of those who had an "A" average are
frequent readers, as compared to 53 percent of those who
had a "C" average.

The percentage of CEOs who read for enjoyment varies considerably from industry to industry. As Table 9–1 shows, all CEOs in the medical products industry frequently read for enjoyment, as compared to only 59 percent of those in retailing.

Given the number of hours involved in a typical work week and the other demands on their time, many CEO booklovers smile at Woody Allen's description of his strategy for fitting reading time into his own hectic schedule. As Allen explains it, "I took a course in speed reading and was able to read *War and Peace* in 20 minutes. It's about Russia."[14]

What Do CEOs Read?

In their book on top management, *Key to the Executive Head*, Otto Lerbinger and Nathaniel H. Sperber found that magazines, especially business and news magazines, take up much of the CEOs' reading time. CEOs are also faithful readers of *The Wall Street Journal* and *The New York*

Table 9–1: Reading for Enjoyment and Industry Goups

Rank	Industry	Percentage of CEOs Who Read Frequently for Enjoyment
1	Medical products	100%
2	Food products	73
3	Manufacturing	70
4	Utilities	70
5	Banking	62
6	Service industries	61
7	Wholesaling	60
8	Transportation	60
9	Retailing	59

Times. No matter what the publication, they usually skip over articles that deal with intellectual or social issues.

According to Lerbinger and Sperber, chief executive officers read about six times more books each year than the national average. Using reading to escape job pressures, CEOs are about twice as likely to read a work of fiction as they are a work on public affairs. Popular favorites include mystery and detective stories, which many CEOs read during business travel. For instance, Mobil's Rawleigh Warner, Jr., favors Travis McGee mystery-adventure books. In this sense, CEOs are not much different from the rest of the population. A Gallup survey for *Publisher's Weekly* revealed that mysteries led the fiction category of book publishers, with some 19 percent of the total.

Recently, *Fortune* magazine asked several CEOs to name the books they had read recently. The list included *Red Storm Rising* by Tom Clancy (William J. Connolly, Jr., of the Bank of New England); *IT* by Stephen King (Richard Furland of Squibb); *Kaisha: The Japanese Corporation* by James C. Abegglen and George Stalk, Jr. (Microsoft's Bill Gates); *The Reckoning* by David Halberstam (Jim Manzi of Lotus Development); and *The Society of Mind* by Marvin Minsky (Apple Computer's John Scully).

But many of the recent choices and lifetime favorites named by the CEOs dealt with business-related topics. Examples included *Ford* by Robert Lacey (Ian Ross of AT&T Bell Laboratories); *Intrapreneuring* by Gifford Pinchot III (Atlantic Richfield's Ladwrick Cook); and Alvin Toffler's *Future Shock* (Philip H. Gaier, Jr., of the Interpublic Group of Cos.).

THE EXERCISE HABITS OF CHIEF EXECUTIVE OFFICERS

Do chief executive officers who have already beaten the competition on the fast track to success spend much time on the athletic track? And how do their exercise routines compare with that of the average American?

An ABC News-*Washington Post* poll gives us insight into how much time Americans spend exercising rigorously. Adult respondents were asked the following question: "Would you say that you exercise strongly for a total of 20 minutes or more a day?" Some 43 percent said they did; 46 percent said they did not; and less than 5 percent had no opinion. Since the survey did not monitor the respondents' actual exercise habits, it is important to remember that individuals may define strong exercise in very different ways. For example, a study of 2,256 middle and top executives at The University of Michigan's Fitness Research Center noted that only 47 percent said they exercised regularly, yet nine out of 10 managers claimed they were in good or excellent shape.

CEOs' Exercise Habits

Four-fifths of today's CEOs have exercise scheduled into their daily regimens. Most stay in shape by playing golf, tennis, or racquetball, or by swimming or jogging. Some of the CEOs who participate in these favorite activities are listed in Table 9–2.

How much time do CEOs devote to keeping in shape? In a survey by executive recruiting firm Howard Sloan Associates, 160 *Fortune* 500 CEOs elaborated on the amount of exercise they do each week. Sixty-nine percent said they exercised between one and five hours each week, 24 percent said six to 10 hours, and 6 percent said they did not exercise at all.

In our study, tennis is the favored activity of those CEOs who come from upper-upper class backgrounds, while golf is favored by those from all other social groups. Those who describe their backgrounds as upper class are more likely to exercise regularly than those from other social backgrounds. While nearly nine out of 10 upper class CEOs exercise regularly, 77 percent of those from middle class backgrounds and 82 percent from lower class backgrounds make this claim. Interestingly, we discovered that a CEO's background as a college athlete seems to have almost no

Table 9–2: How Some CEOs Get Their Exercise

Tennis Players	Golfers	Racquetball Players	Joggers	Swimmers
Lewis Preston Morgan Guaranty Trust Company of New York	Robert Mercer Goodyear Tire & Rubber Company	T. Boone Pickens, Jr. Mesa Petroleum Company	Stewart Turley Jack Eckerd Corporation	Richard Smith General Cinema Corporation
Charles Harper Con Agra, Inc,	Fred Hartley Unocal Corporation	Richard Eamer National Medical Enterprises, Inc.	Roland Trafton Safeco Corporation	Robert Galvin Motorola
Sidney Peterson Getty Oil Company	Alexander Giacco Hercules, Inc.	William Emmet Wall Kansas Power and Light	Don Calvin Frisbee Pacific Power & Light	John Breen Sherwin Williams
Paul Oreffice Dow Chemical Company	Richard Zimmerman Hershey Foods Corporation	Michael Wright Super Valu Stores	Thomas Frist Hospital Corporation of America	John Fisher Nationwide Insurance
Richard Gordon McGovern Campbell Soup Company	Kenneth Macke Dayton Hudson Corporation	Paul Hensen United Tele-Communications, Inc.	Charles Edward Sporck National Semi Corporation	John Doyle Ong B.F. Goodrich
Jack Rowe Minnesota Power	John McKinney Manville Corporation	Frank Manaut Bank of Hawaii, Inc.	Frank Luenssen Inland Steel	Warren Earl McCain Albertson's, Inc.
Raymond Zimmerman Service Merchandise	Albert Casey American Airlines	John Hall Ashland Oil	Gordon E. Crosby, Jr. U.S. Life Corporation	George Butler First Pennsylvania Bank
Arthur Seder, Jr. American Natural Resources	Rand Araskog ITT	Morton Meyerson EDS	James Berrett Computervision	T.J. Barlow Anderson Clayton
Bud Grossman Gelco Corporation	Louis Bantle U.S. Tobacco	Jerry Douglas Geist Public Service of New Mexico	Sam Seynar Internorth	J. Peter Grace W.R. Grace & Co.
Roy Anderson Lockheed Corp.	Robert Charpie Cabot Corporation	Forrest Shumway Signal	Donald Lennox International Harvester	William Marquard American Standard

relationship to his current exercise habits. Approximately 80 percent of those who played sports in college now exercise—about the same percentage as those who did not participate in intercollegiate athletics.

A connection also exists between industry affiliation and the exercise habits and choice of sports of chief executives. When viewed on an industry-by-industry basis, the percentages of those who exercise regularly vary enormously. Those most likely to exercise are in the transportation industry; in fact, every respondent in this group claims that exercise is a part of his regular routine. The CEOs with the poorest showing are in the medical products industry, with only 25 percent saying that they exercise regularly. Table 9–3 ranks the exercise habits of the CEOs of nine industries.

Table 9–3: Exercise Patterns and Industry Groups

Rank	Industry	Percentage of CEOs Who Exercise
1	Transportation	100%
2	Service industries	89
3	Manufacturing	83
4	Utilities	81
5	Banking	76
6	Retailing	65
7	Food products	64
8	Wholesaling	60
9	Medical products	25

When we looked at the sports preferences of the CEOs, definite industry patterns emerged. Here are some of our findings.
- Wholesaling has the greatest concentration of golfers (eight out of ten play), and service industries the smallest number (46 percent).
- Most joggers come from the service industries (34 percent), while there are none in the medical products field.
- CEOs in the medical products field participate in swimming more than CEOs in any other industry group. CEOs in the wholesaling field are least likely to engage in this activity.

- Racquetball, the least popular sport among today's chief executive officers, has no participants in the retailing, medical products, and food products fields. With a 20 percent participation rate, CEOs in the wholesaling industry play racquetball more frequently than top executives in any other group.

What Makes CEOs Exercise?

With an 80 percent overall participation rate, chief executive officers clearly value exercise as a part of their daily routines. Some who were athletes in college draw a connection between the lessons learned on the playing field and the successes they have achieved in their business careers. Mesa Petroleum chairman T. Boone Pickens, Jr. draws this comparison: "We were the underdogs in most of the deals we've been in, but we never panicked. In sports, I found you can be behind and come back."[15]

Many CEOs exercise because of the connection between exercise and health. Realizing that exercise may help reduce the risk of heart attack and high blood pressure, many top executives have made a conscious decision to exercise regularly as a way of taking responsibility for their own health. To keep fit, octogenarian Armand Hammer, the chairman of Occidental Petroleum, swims half an hour daily in his backyard pool. William Bricker, chairman of Diamond Shamrock, takes long walks.

Some corporate leaders, like Pepsico chairman Donald Kendall, are fortunate enough to be able to exercise right at work. Kendall jogs every day on the track built at the company's Purchase, New York corporate headquarters. GTE chairman Theodore Brophy works out on the company's rowing machines, treadmills, and Nautilus equipment. At most corporate health facilities, exercise specialists are on hand to make sure that managers get the most benefit from exercise time.

Whether exercise helps CEOs deal with stress or whether they are constitutionally well suited to deal with it in the first place is open to question. "I think the capacity to handle stress is part of the personality make-up of most executives," says Dr. Joseph Panella, medical director of Mobil Corporation. "There are very strong pressures all the way up the corporate ladder."[16] Dr. Granville Walker, medical director of Chase Manhattan Corporation, agrees. "There is job stress, family stress, even commutation stress. But this condition is not necessarily harmful to executive health."[17]

When Dun's *Business Month* asked more than 200 CEOs if stress had hurt their health, only three said they saw their job stress as harmful. On the contrary, the vast majority saw work-related stress as a good thing. "The CEO's job is not stressful if he is in charge of himself," commented one panelist. "A blue-collar worker who is not secure has much greater stress." Texaco chairman John K. McKinley adds, "Putting in long hours for many days in a row without much time off is more tiring than stressful."[18] Interestingly, workaholism, which seems to be a defining characteristic of many chief executive officers, is not considered hazardous to their health. A person who is happy at his work, no matter how many hours he puts in, is not likely to experience the negative effects of stress.

THE MUSICAL TASTES OF CHIEF EXECUTIVE OFFICERS

"I want to have music everywhere I go,"[19] says Sony chairman Akio Morita, who claims that music is the driving force in his life. Morita listens to a Walkman while he skis, and to a compact disk player while his chauffer drives. He has more than 200 speakers in his home. Though his favorite is classical music, the 65-year-old also enjoys the vibrations of the younger set: he likes going to Billy Joel and Bruce Springsteen concerts.

While music may not dominate their lives as it does Morita's, nearly all chief executive officers enjoy listening to music. At the top of their lists of favorites are classical and easy-listening music; more than half of the CEOs listen to both. They listen to other types of music far less frequently: one in six listens to country and western music; 9 percent, opera; 5 percent, soft rock; 2 percent, bluegrass; and only one CEO prefers hard rock. Who tunes in to what type of music? Thomas Macioa of Allied Stores Group is an opera buff. Soft rock fans include James Berrett of Computervision and Jesse Aweida of Storage Technology. Donald Petersen of Ford Motor Co. listens to jazz on Detroit station WJZZ.

Social Class Background Makes a Difference

CEOs coming from middle class backgrounds show a definite preference for classical music; two-thirds of those from lower-middle class and 57 percent of those from upper-middle class backgrounds say they enjoy listening to classical music. Interestingly, those CEOs from the middle class have an even stronger preference for classical music than do those reared in upper class backgrounds. Those from upper-lower class backgrounds also express a stronger preference for classical music than those from the upper

Table 9–4: Social Class and Music Preferences

| Type of Music | Social Class Background | | |
	Upper	Middle	Lower
Easy listening	67%	56%	59%
Classical	50	60	57
Country and western	11	15	28
Opera	11	9	8
Soft rock	—	7	8
Bluegrass	—	2	3

Note: Totals may not add to 100 percent due to multiple responses.

classes. CEOs from a lower-lower class background, however, do not share this musical taste. More than half prefer country and western music, as compared to 25 percent who favor classical music. Table 9–4 presents the type of music chief executive officers listen to, classified by social background.

Music Preferences Vary by Industry

While all CEOs in the medical products industry listen to classical music, only about one-third of those in retailing do so. CEOs in the medical products field also enjoy opera and soft rock more than CEOs in any other industry group. Table 9–5 presents the listening habits of chief executive officers according to industry affiliation.

Table 9–5: Industry Group and Music Preference

| | Types of Music | | | |
Industry	Classical	Country/ Western	Opera	Soft Rock
Medical products	100%	25%	25%	25%
Transportation	70	30	10	—
Utilities	70	12	12	5
Service industries	63	20	2	5
Manufacturing	57	17	7	3
Food products	55	9	9	—
Banking	51	16	7	7
Wholesaling	40	40	20	—
Retailing	35	17	18	—

Note: Totals may not add to 100 percent due to multiple responses.

SUMMING UP

Most of today's CEOs read and listen to music for pleasure, and exercise to stay in shape. Clearly, some CEOs define their lives almost completely in terms of their work. The comment of one CEO makes this apparent: "The pressure and stress of my job are what keep me alive. I can't think of a quicker way to unhealth than to be home doing nothing."[20] Others attribute career success to a fuller life. When asked if he would change anything about his life, Paul Oreffice replied, "Nothing different! A balanced life is the secret. Also very important is the ability to engage in activities that allow you to forget the problems of the day."[21]

Whether or not CEOs choose to give themselves leisure time and to pursue nonwork activities that give them pleasure depends to a great extent on personal makeup and priorities. Edmund T. Pratt, Jr., of Pfizer, Inc., puts it this way, "There's a balancing act that goes on in every person's career, of balancing the different pulls one feels from many directions. Family versus career. Career versus other activities that you're interested in."[22] While important to some and not to others, leisure is clearly an issue for all top executives.

———■———

1. Terry McDermott, "Shrontz: Taking Over at Boeing," *The Seattle Times/Seattle Post-Intelligencer,* 2 March 1986, D1, D8.
2. "All in the Family Fortune," *Time Magazine,* 22 September 1986, 74.
3. Ralph Nader and William Taylor, *The Big Boys* (New York: Pantheon Books, 1986), 155.
4. Barbara Rowes, *The Book of Quotes* (New York: Ballantine Books, 1987), 18.
5. Some of the following material is based on a forthcoming article by the authors in *American Demographer.* Used with permission.
6. "Labor Letter," *The Wall Street Journal,* 5 August 1986, 1.
7. Charles Downey, "All Worked Up Over Work," *American Way,* 5 February 1985, 85–89.

8. Ibid.
9. Arnold Ehrlich, "Workaholism—A Rampant Malady," *Forbes*, 20 July 1981, 20.
10. Beth Brophy, "Workaholics Beware: Long Hours May Not Pay," *U.S. News & World Report*, 7 April 1986, 60.
11. Ehrlich, 20.
12. Brophy, 60.
13. "The Art of Managers," *Across the Board*, July/August 1985, 40.
14. Robert Byrne, *The Other 637 Best Things Anybody Ever Said* (New York: Atheneum, 1985), 568.
15. John A. Byrne, "Executive Sweat," *Forbes*, 20 May 1985, 200.
16. John Perham, "Executive Health Audit," *Dun's Business Month*, October 1984, 92.
17. Ibid., 104.
18. "How Busy CEOs Keep In Shape, *Dun's Business Month*, October 1984, 104.
19. John Hillkirk, "Akio Morita," *USA Today*, 29 October 1986, 4B.
20. Perham, 106.
21. Ibid.
22. Edmund T. Pratt, Jr., interviewed by David Finn, *Across the Board*, December 1985, 37.

"I view myself as, No. 1, the person responsible to get the right people and make sure they have the tools to do the job."

John Ellis, CEO
Puget Sound Power and Light[1]

10

MANAGEMENT STYLES

The management styles of American CEOs are as diverse as their personalities. But regardless of the approaches they use to run their firms, most share the common trait of working hard.

Sam Walton of Wal-Mart is a hands-on manager. He tours his stores so frequently that he is on a first name basis with thousands of employees. His success has made him one of the very few billionaires in the United States.

Work so dominated the life of H. J. Haynes that when he retired as Chevron's CEO, he had accumulated 19 months of vacation. During his last two years on the job, Haynes spent only six weekends at home.

When asked if he was a workaholic, Puget Power's CEO John Ellis commented, "I am, but not by the normal definition. I don't choose to be a workaholic, but I think the demands of the job are such that you certainly follow the schedule of a workaholic. That doesn't mean there aren't times I wouldn't rather be doing something else."[2] Sometimes Ellis does exactly that . . . he flies, skis, sails, plays tennis, and even plays in a small band.

ORGANIZERS VERSUS MANAGERS

Some of today's CEOs essentially created their companies, either founding them or crafting them into their present forms through mergers and acquisitions. Charles G. Burck of *Fortune* magazine called these CEOs the organizers. The remainder can be called professional administrators, or simply managers. According to Burck's 1976 study of *Fortune* 500 chief executives, the proportion of organizers among CEOs has changed considerably during this century. In 1900, about 30 percent of top executives categorized themselves as organizers. By 1950, the figure had fallen to about 5 percent. At the time of his study, Burck reported that this proportion had about doubled, due to the rise of conglomerates and companies that were the result of mergers.

THE BEST OF THE BEST

Benjamin Franklin divided people into three classes: those who are immovable; those who are movable; and those who move. Every corporate employee, manager, and stockholder hopes that his firm's CEO falls into the latter class. But who are the best CEOs, and what makes them the best? Several years ago, *Fortune* surveyed the chief executive officers of its top 500 companies concerning who they thought were the best CEOs and the best-managed companies. The runaway winner was Reginald Jones, the CEO of General Electric, who garnered 164 votes. John Swearingen of Standard Oil of Indiana (and later Continental Illinois), the number two vote-getter, had only 10 votes.

What were the qualities that won Jones the plaudits of his peers? One of the most prominent was his unstinting effort to develop managerial talent and foster an entrepreneurial spirit by giving the managers of GE's small subunits as much freedom as possible to run their operations.

John Swearingen also was lauded for his efforts to give autonomy and responsibility to those lower in the corporate hierarchy. "It's important for people to be able to spend a certain amount of money on their own, and be answerable for it after the fact,"[3] he maintains. By allowing this to happen, Standard of Indiana puts its money where its mouth is.

More recently, a study by Heidrick & Struggles failed to produce a majority choice for the nation's most effective CEO. However, the CEOs cited most often were General Electric's John Welch; Roy Vogelos of Merck & Co.; and Chrysler's Lee Iacocca. All exhibit qualities similar to those of Jones and Swearingen.

SOME FAIL, TOO

Not all CEOs are successful in their fields. Some, like William Agee, former chairman of Bendix Corporation, seem to sabotage themselves. Business consultants give several major causes of CEO failure.

In some cases, failure results from poor decisions resulting from an inability to anticipate change. A recent advertisement by United Technologies Corporation listed several glaring blunders:

> An irate banker demanded that Alexander Graham Bell remove "that toy" from his office. That toy was the telephone. A Hollywood producer scrawled a rejection note on a manuscript that became *Gone with the Wind*. Henry Ford's largest original investor sold all his stock in 1906. Roebuck sold out to Sears for $25,000 in 1895. Today, Sears may sell $25,000 of goods in 16 seconds.

Insensitivity is one of the most common problems plaguing top executives. This problem ranges from not sharing time with subordinates to, in its worst manifestation, belittling them in public. A CEO's insensitivity can create an atmosphere in which employees do not perform up to their abilities; and, as a result, the firm's overall performance suffers. Arrogance is a related frequent personality flaw. However, insensitivity is usually connected to other problems when it causes the downfall of the executive.

Some CEOs' problems begin when they get so used to hearing words of praise, but little or no criticism, that they start believing what they are told about themselves. They then act on it, sometimes trying to achieve the impossible.

Another common flaw among chief executives is indecisiveness, often a cover for insecurity. By delaying too long in making a choice, they lose control over events. The CEO's indecisiveness may also result in his trying to move both ways on an issue, completely muddling the company's direction. If this flaw is combined with poor foresight, the result can be devastating financial losses such as those suffered by many computer firms when they overestimated the market for home computers.

Being a bad judge of people can be the most costly of a CEO's problems. As Roderick Heller, CEO of Bristol Compressors, puts it, "The CEO is really a high-level personnel person."[4] If good management training is the hallmark of the best CEOs, a lack of it is one of the surest signs of a CEO's failure to provide for the company in the long run.

Another reason some CEOs fail is that they cannot adjust to their positions. Some find it hard to handle power. Others miss the immediate gratification they received from their work when they were at lower levels of the hierarchy. In either case, their performance is not what was expected based on their previous accomplishments. Still other CEOs cannot handle failure. Often, they will stay on past the time they should have left the company.

ATTITUDES TOWARD CHANGE

A manager's attitude toward change can affect his company's fortunes. M. J. Kirton and Glenn Mulligan conducted a study in which they examined managers' attitudes toward change in general and toward change in employee evaluation procedures in particular. They found that managerial status was not related to attitude toward change in general, but it was strongly correlated with attitude toward changes in employee appraisal schemes. The latter was considered a common sense finding: top-level managers were more receptive to such changes than lower level managers since they had already "made it" and had nothing to risk.

This finding is also consistent with earlier findings that those who control change are more receptive to it than those who have it imposed upon them. As they expected, Kirton and Mulligan found that older managers were less receptive to change on both general and specific measures. They also reconfirmed earlier findings that the better educated managers were more receptive to change in general; but they found virtually no correlation between education and attitude toward the specific promotion policy, which they suggested might treat the educated in a preferential fashion.

Several personality variables also showed significant correlations with attitudes toward change. Managers' confidence in themselves and in the jobs they were doing was positively related to both change in general and changes in the appraisal scheme in particular. In addition, both contentment and frustration correlated positively with a favorable attitude toward the appraisal scheme, while those neither strongly contented nor frustrated were generally opposed to it.

EARLIER RESEARCH ON THE JOB TRAITS OF CEOs

Over a decade ago, Otto Lerbinger and Nathaniel H. Sperber compiled a list of the professional traits of CEOs. Their characterization follows:

1. They have "exhibited drive and creativity," and they "agree that leaders ought to be both perceptive and enthusiastic."
2. They are not very communicative. (Despite this, Burck's study for *Fortune* magazine found that CEOs did not think they needed any special training in communication or public speaking.)
3. They do not rate imagination or concentration very highly.

4. Parallel with the second point, they do not think it is very important to get along with their co-workers.
5. As a result, CEOs are very often secretive and impersonal. Thus they are often seen as dictatorial.[5]

WHAT ABOUT TODAY'S CEOs?

To begin our investigation of the managerial styles of today's CEOs, we asked them to rank themselves on a scale of 1 to 3 reflecting their organization or lack of it. On this scale, 1 is organized, 2 is median and 3 is disorganized. Almost half of the respondents (44 percent) see themselves as organized, another large group (40 percent) rank themselves in the middle, and only 13 percent admit being disorganized.

Social Class is Linked to Organization

Social class generally correlates positively with organization. From the upper-upper to lower-middle class, the percentage of well organized CEOs declines; then there is a rise in organization among the upper-lower class, and a huge rise among the lower-lower class, as Table 10–1 shows.

The figure that stands out is the 100 percent of lower-lower class respondents who say they are well organized. This is perhaps one way in which those who come from less privileged backgrounds are able to make up for a disadvantaged beginning.

Transportation and Wholesaling CEOs Are the Best Organized

A breakdown of the data reveals substantial variation among industries. Transportation and wholesaling have the highest percentages of CEOs who describe themselves as highly organized, while medical products and utilities have

Table 10-1: Social Class and Degree of Organization

Social Class Background	Degree of Organization		
	Organized	Median	Disorganized
Upper-upper	89%	11%	—
Lower-upper	50	25	25%
Upper-middle	45	34	15
Lower-middle	29	58	8
Upper-lower	39	52	9
Lower-lower	100	—	—

Note: Totals may not add to 100 percent due to rounding and nonresponses.

the lowest proportions. There were no median scores on organization among wholesaling executives; they were either organized or disorganized. Table 10–2 gives the complete results.

The Parental Connection

Two-parent families, we found, produced both more organized and more disorganized CEOs, with CEOs from one-parent families tending toward the median. Of the CEOs reared by a single parent, 38 percent say they are well organized, 48 percent fall in the median, and 5 percent are disorganized. For those coming from a two-parent background, 45 percent are in the well organized category, 39 percent in the median, and 14 percent in the disorganized group.

Table 10-2: Industry Group and Degree of Organization

Industry	Degree of Organization		
	Organized	Median	Disorganized
Transportation	60%	30%	10%
Wholesaling	60	—	40
Banking	56	29	9
Service industries	46	44	2
Manufacturing	39	39	15
Food products	36	36	27
Retailing	35	41	18
Utilities	26	58	14
Medical products	25	75	—

Note: Totals may not add to 100 percent due to rounding and nonresponses.

THE ELEMENT OF HUMOR

Having a good sense of humor is an asset shared by most CEOs. We reached this conclusion in Chapter 3, where our data showed that 60 percent of all CEOs said their friends and family consider them humorous, and another 35 percent thought their associates consider them moderately humorous.

Table 10-3: Humor and Verbal/Numerical Abilities

Ability	Humorous	Moderately Humorous	Humorless
Numerical	50%	41%	7%
Verbal	62	34	4
Equal	77	18	5

A survey by Robert Half International, Inc., found that a vast majority of executives believe that workers with a good sense of humor do a better job than those without one. A third of those surveyed, the highest proportion on this question, also said that top management had the greatest concentration of people with a good sense of humor. Our data support this.

Humor Is Linked to Verbal/Numerical Ability

We found that CEOs with better verbal ability are more humorous than those who excel at numbers. Funnier than both of these groups, however, are those equally adept in both verbal and numerical skills, as Table 10-3 indicates.

It probably should not surprise us that "verbals" are funnier than "numericals;" but the position of the "equals" is surprising, both at the top (the highest percentage of humorous CEOs) and the bottom (exceeding the "verbals" on being humorless). The latter would not be anomalous if it occurred alone, but in the context of outperfecting the "verbals" it is puzzling.

Are Laterborn CEOs More Humorous Than Firstborns?

It appears that there is a slight tendency for those born later in a family to be more humorous than those born earlier. Firstborns have the highest percentage of humorless respondents. The secondborn are at the top of our humor scale. However, it should be noted that the relationship between birth order and humor, if it exists, is very weak.

The Connection Between Humor and the Name Used by CEOs

The name used by a CEO has a stronger connection to humor than does his birth order. CEOs who go by their initials are much more likely to consider themselves humorous. By contrast, those going by their nicknames are most likely to consider themselves humorless.

Why CEOs using their initials should be funnier is mystifying, since one might expect that those with nicknames would be funnier as a result of their family lives (recall the discussion on birth order and nicknames, where we found that middle children are relatively disadvantaged and typically called by their first or middle names).

Food Products CEOs Can Be a Serious Lot

Among industries, transportation clearly has the funniest CEOs, while food products has the highest proportion of humorless executives. The humor rankings for CEOs of each industry are detailed in Table 10–4.

Table 10–4: Humor and Industry Group

Industry	Humorous	Moderately Humorous	Humorless
Transportation	78%	22%	—
Banking	66	30	2%
Manufacturing	60	36	4
Utilities	59	31	10
Service industries	58	39	3
Medical products	50	50	—
Retailing	46	46	8
Food products	40	40	20
Wholesaling	40	60	—

Note: Totals may not add to 100 percent due to rounding.

CREATIVITY

Creativity is an important characteristic of successful managers. Just over half of all CEOs consider themselves creative, and only one in 12 rates himself as unimaginative.

In analyzing our data, we found that the most creative CEOs are laterborn children, go by their initials, are better with words than numbers or are equally good at both, held an office in a college club, and head firms in the medical products industry.

Supporting other research findings, our data show that laterborn children tend to be the more creative. Three in five of the CEOs born fourth or later score high on creativity. The proportion decreases steadily for the third- and secondborn, down to one in two of the firstborn who considers himself creative.

CEOs who go by their initials are not only the most humorous, but also the most creative of our respondents. None of the initialed CEOs thinks of himself as unimaginative. Those who use their first names have the lowest proportion in the creative category, and the highest percentage in the unimaginative category.

In another striking analogy to humor, we found that CEOs with better verbal than numerical ability tend to be more creative. Only one "numerical" in three considers himself creative, while almost 60 percent of the "verbals" do so. But outranking even the "verbals" are those who are equal on both abilities: four-fifths of them say they are creative.

It comes as no surprise that CEOs who held an office in a college club or other group score higher on creativity than those who did not hold an office. Of the office holders, 55 percent see themselves as creative, while only 45 percent of the non-officeholders do so.

In assessing creativity among industries, we found that CEOs in medical products are the most creative, while those in wholesaling and retailing are the least imaginative. Of the medical products CEOs, 75 percent say they are creative. At the low end, only 46 percent of retailing CEOs see themselves as creative. In the other industries, between 50 and 60 percent of the CEOs fall in the creative category. The highest percentages of unimaginative CEOs are in wholesaling (20 percent) and retailing (15 percent). Not one CEO in food products, medical products, or the service industries considers himself unimaginative.

THE CORRELATES OF NUMERICAL AND VERBAL ABILITY

As we reported in an earlier chapter, most chief executives feel that they are better in verbal ability than in numerical ability, and about 10 percent report that they are equal in the two areas. "Verbals" make up about 58 percent, and "numericals" 32 percent.

Some CEOs report that their numerical and verbal orientations are sometimes in conflict. Roger Enrico of Pepsi-Cola has remarked, "I raced through college in three years, so busy running a fraternity and the student court and editing the yearbook that I never really decided what I'd do afterward. I was good at numbers—not advanced math, just plain old simple numbers—but I really wanted to do something that was more people-oriented."[6] Like most people who rise to the CEO level, Enrico was able to resolve this conflict.

Verbal Ability Is Related to Degree of Organization and Creativity

In the analysis of our data, we found that CEOs who rate higher on verbal ability than numerical ability show a slight superiority in being well organized. But those equal in their verbal/numerical abilities have the highest percentage of organized people.

When we looked at the likelihood of people being "verbals" or "numericals" as a function of their creativity or lack thereof, we found that the creative CEOs are more likely than average to be better at verbal ability. They are also more likely to be equal in the two kinds of ability.

Firstborn CEOs Have the Best Numerical Abilities

Birth order is also associated with relative numerical or verbal ability. Simply stated, the earlier in his family a CEO was born, the more likely it is that he has more numerical ability. Conversely, the later a CEO was born in his family,

Table 10–5: Verbal/Numerical Abilities and Birth Order

Birth Order	Numerical	Verbal	Equal
First	44%	45%	12%
Second	26	61	12
Third	23	71	6
Fourth or later	15	75	10

Note: Totals may not add to 100 percent due to rounding.

the more likely he is to have a greater verbal ability. Table 10–5 breaks down this information.

The Parental Link to Numerical/Verbal Abilities

The CEO's number of parents has a slight impact on his numerical or verbal ability. Interestingly, all three respondents who had one parent part-time or two parents part-time report that they are equal in numerical and verbal abilities. CEOs who had one parent are considerably more likely than average to be better in verbal ability (67 percent versus the 58 percent average), while those from two-parent households are just slightly more likely than average to be better at numerical ability (33 percent versus 32 percent).

J. R. Ewing Is Probably a Good Numbers Man

The name used by the CEO clearly correlates with numerical versus verbal ability. Those using a nickname are more likely to be "verbals" or "equals," while those going by their initials are more likely to excel at numerical tasks.

Interestingly, those using both their first and middle names are more likely than average to be numerically oriented. In the case of middle name users, they are more likely to be "verbals," but less likely to be "equals."

The "Verbals" Were Big Men on Campus

Extracurricular activity in college correlates with verbal ability. Both those who started a business or club and those who held an office are more likely than average to be better at verbal ability than numerical ability. For the entrepreneurs, the difference is quite large: 70 percent versus 58 percent. For the office holders, the difference is miniscule: less than 1 percent.

The CEO's Industry Makes a Difference

Finally, there are major differences in the verbal and numerical abilities of CEOs as classified by industry. The medical products industry has the highest percentage of "verbals" and no "numericals," while transportation has the highest percentage of "numericals," and services has the highest proportion of "equals." As Table 10–6 shows, manufacturing and retailing have a high number of

---

Table 10–6: Verbal/Numerical Abilities and Industry Group

Industry	Numerical	Verbal	Equal
Transportation	50%	40%	10%
Retailing	47	41	12
Manufacturing	41	50	9
Food products	36	55	9
Service industries	29	54	17
Banking	27	64	7
Utilities	23	63	14
Wholesaling	20	80	—
Medical products	—	100	—

Note: Totals may not add to 100 percent due to rounding.

---

numerically-oriented CEOs, while banking, wholesaling, and utilities have considerably higher than average levels of "verbals."

LEADERSHIP STYLE

In management literature, writers usually refer to three types of leadership styles: Theory X, in which the leader makes all the important decisions himself; Theory Y, a participative approach in which lower level employees make important contributions to the decision making process; and Theory Z, in which the leader seeks a consensus on goals and methods of meeting them.

The Theory Y participative leadership style is the prevalent approach of most CEOs of America's top corporations. This approach is favored by four-fifths of today's corporate leaders. One CEO, Hugh A. Barker of Public Service Indiana, comments that he is "conscientiously seeking to alter my company (and my own) style from autocratic to participative." Barker's new style is anything but new. Lao Tzu, in 600 B.C., described a Theory Y manager thusly:

> A manager is best when people barely know that he exists. Not so good when people obey and acclaim him. Worse when they despise him. Fail to honor people, they fail to honor you. But of a good manager, who talks little, when his work is done, his aim fulfilled, they will all say, "we did this ourselves."

One CEO in ten states a preference for Theory X, and 4 percent prefer Theory Z. A small percentage of today's executives use a combination of the approaches.

CEO Longevity Has an Impact on Leadership Style

One factor clearly affecting a CEO's choice of leadership style is his length of tenure in office. Those who have been a CEO for longer periods are much more likely to use Theory X than are other respondents; similarly, they are less likely to use Theory Y. But those who have been a CEO

for 20 or more years are the most likely to use Theory Z.
Table 10–7 illustrates these points.

Table 10–7: Leadership Style and Employment Tenure

Years as CEO	Theory X	Theory Y	Theory Z	X&Y/Y&Z	X&Y&Z
1	3%	86%	7%	3%	—
2 to 3	9	86	3	3	—
4 to 5	11	85	—	4	—
6 to 7	7	87	3	—	—
8 to 10	10	81	7	3	—
11 to 13	16	76	—	8	—
14 to 19	13	77	4	4	4%
20 or more	20	60	13	7	—

Note: Totals may not add to 100 percent due to rounding.

Industry Affiliation Has an Impact on Leadership Style

Variation in leadership styles among CEOs of different
industries is substantial. Retailing has the highest percentage of Theory X people, with 29 percent. Theory Y is
adhered to by all the wholesaling respondents. And utilities
and food products CEOs are the most likely to use Theory
Z, but even here the proportion is small—9 percent (Table
10–8).

It is important to note that these are the predominant
leadership styles used by these CEOs. It is rare to find any
leader who relies totally upon a single approach, because
different situations call for different styles.

J. Clayton Lafferty, President of Human Synergistics,
Inc., offers a telling illustration of the need for flexibility in
meeting unexpected developments.

When a three-engine Boeing 727, flying at 40,000 feet, loses
all three engines at once (under normal circumstances the

plane could glide for over 130 miles), the captain has ample time for quickly consulting with his copilot and flight engineer to get their ideas about the cause and remedy, and to discuss emergency procedures with the stewardesses. However, if a similar power loss occurred at 500 feet during a takeoff climb, the captain would be ill advised to practice such participative techniques.[7]

Table 10–8: Leadership Style and Industry Groups

Industry	Theory X	Theory Y	Theory Z	Others
Retailing	29%	71%	—	—
Medical products	25	75	—	—
Transportation	20	70	—	10%
Manufacturing	11	80	2%	8
Banking	7	84	4	5
Service industries	7	85	2	5
Utilities	5	84	9	2
Food products	—	91	9	—
Wholesaling	—	100	—	—

Note: Totals may not add to 100 percent due to rounding.

Theory X Managers Tend to be Number Crunchers, Good Organizers, and Ivy Leaguers

One interesting finding is that those CEOs who are stronger in numerical ability than in verbal ability are much more likely than average to use Theory X, with almost 20 percent for the "numericals" as opposed to about 7 percent for the "verbals," and only about 4 percent for the "equals."

Those CEOs who consider themselves very organized are more likely than average to use Theory X. Indeed, they are more than twice as likely to use it than are the disorganized respondents, and three times more likely to do so than the median respondents.

College choice has its role, too, with Ivy Leaguers being the most likely to use Theory X (14 percent), followed by private and public schoolers at 8 percent each.

Analyzing another aspect of CEOs' college backgrounds, we found that those who had held office in a club or organization are less likely to use Theory X than are those who had not (8 percent versus 13 percent). At the same time, they are much less likely to use Theory Z (2 percent versus 9 percent).

One Final Classification

Finally, we found that those chief executives who go by their first names are much less likely to use Theory X than anyone else. Those using their middle names or initials are more than twice as likely as those using first names to use Theory X, and those using a nickname are almost twice as likely to do so.

CEO DECISION MAKING

With whom do CEOs consult when they make decisions? Three-fourths of today's corporate leaders depend upon the input of trusted associates. Less than one in seven CEOs make major managerial decisions alone, and about 3 percent turn to outsiders for consultation.

In parallel with leadership style, it is clearly the case that CEOs who have held their positions longer tend to be more closed-mouthed, consulting only themselves. Indeed, fully one-third of those who have been CEO for 20 years or longer do so. Interestingly, first-year CEOs also have a fairly high tendency to keep their own counsel, with 14 percent doing so. Though consulting with outsiders is not common in any category, it is concentrated among chief executives who have been in their positions for over six years. We also found that the relatively creative tend to rely more on themselves than do those who are unimaginative.

Other Classifications of CEO Decision Making Styles

Creative CEOs tend more toward self-reliance when making decisions than do those who are less imaginative. On the other hand, organization/orderliness has little relationship with who is consulted. What little trend there is suggests that the disorganized are slightly more likely to consult themselves than are the well organized CEOs, but it is only a matter of 15 percent to 12 percent.

Those who held office in college apparently learned to cooperate in making decisions, since they are more likely to consult with others than are the non-office holders. Again, the difference is small, with 12 percent of the office holders saying they consult themselves only, as opposed to 15 percent of the non-office holders doing so.

A slightly larger difference arises between corporate leaders coming from one-parent and two-parent households. The CEOs from two-parent households are more likely to keep things to themselves, with 14 percent of them reporting that they consult only themselves, while just 10 percent of the respondents from one-parent households do so.

SUMMING UP

Not surprisingly, the vast majority of today's CEOs claim to be orderly and organized. Only about one out of eight admits to being disorganized. Social class is slightly correlated (positively) with organization. Of all industries, transportation and wholesaling possess executives who are the most organized, while medical products and utilities have the lowest percentage of well organized executives.

About three-fifths also claim to be humorous. "Verbals" are more likely to be humorous than "numericals," but those equal in the two areas score highest of all for humor. A very weak relationship between humor and birth order may exist, but this requires further research to confirm. CEOs using their initials have the highest humor score, though the reasons for this are unclear. A clearer connection arises between industry and humor, with transportation executives being the most humorous and those in food products the least funny.

Even fewer CEOs admit to being low in creativity than low in organization; only one in 12. Again, the laterborn, those using their initials, "verbals" and "equals," and those who held offices in college score better than average on creativity. Medical products has the most creative people, and wholesaling and retailing the least creative.

The typical CEO ranks higher in verbal ability than in numerical ability (58 percent versus 32 percent), with about 10 percent equal in both abilities. Creativity and verbal ability tend to go together, as do being firstborn and possessing numerical ability. The number of parents a CEO grew up with had little impact. Those using a nickname have the highest percentage of both "verbals" and "equals," while those using their initials are the most likely to be stronger in numerical ability. Medical products CEOs have the highest proportion of "verbals;" transportation, the most "numericals;" and service industries, the greatest percentage of "equals."

Leadership style and decision making exhibit similar patterns of responses. Theory Y is the most common leadership style, and consulting with trusted associates the most common decision making approach. Long-time CEOs are most likely to use Theory X and to consult only themselves. Retail executives are most likely to use Theory X, wholesalers Theory Y, and utilities CEOs Theory Z. "Numericals" and Ivy Leaguers are also more likely to use Theory X. Organized behavior is closely connected to Theory X, but has little relationship to decision making. Those who held office in college are more likely to consult with others, and less likely to use Theory X. CEOs going by their first names are the least likely to use Theory X. Finally, we found that creative CEOs are more likely than average to consult only themselves when making important decisions.

1. Terry McDermott, "The Cream of the Corporate Crop," *Pacific,* 10 August 1986, 5. A publication of *The Seattle Times/Seattle Post Intelligencer.*
2. Ibid.
3. Ann M. Morrison, "CEOs Pick the Best CEOs," *Fortune,* 4 May 1981, 134.
4. Bruce Horowitz, "Why Some CEOs Fail," *Industry Week,* 31 October 1983, 97.
5. Otto Lerbinger and Nathaniel H. Sperber, *Key to the Executive Head* (Reading, Massachusetts: Addison-Wesley Publishing Co., 1975), 123.
6. Roger Enrico, "Follow Me! The Path of a Leader," *Across the Board,* January 1987, 24.
7. Lafferty is quoted in Dale D. McConkey, "Participative Management: What it Really Means in Practice," *Business Horizons,* October 1980, 68.

EPILOGUE

After numerous pages and examples describing every aspect of the CEO's life history, career pattern, sense of humor, and anatomy, one has the right to ask: What does it all mean? How does it all fit together into a composite portrait of the leaders of corporate America?

The information collected in the course of preparing this portrait of America's business leaders was voluminous, varied, and sometimes maddening as we sought to extract insights from the data. Literally dozens of computer runs assisted in locating truths from the input of over 200 corporate chieftains. What emerged from the study is a comprehensive and detailed profile of the nation's top executives. Let's summarize our findings.

THE PROFILE THAT EMERGED

The following profile of our CEOs emerged:

⟹ CEOs were born and raised by two-parent families in what is now called the "Rust Belt."

⟹ CEOs typically have two siblings. Over 44 percent of our CEOs are firstborns.

⟹ Over 50 percent of today's CEOs are from upper-middle class backgrounds. However, there is considerable divergence among CEOs of different industries. Interestingly, banking has the highest proportion of CEOs from lower-lower class backgrounds.

➤ CEOs are taller than the national average, and most of them would be considered physically fit. They are also usually attractive, and are right-handed.

➤ Our CEOs are healthier than is the general population. As a result, they sleep less than the medical profession's standard recommendation. It is also significant to note that the CEO is considerably less likely to smoke than is the average American male.

➤ A stable marriage—with a median length of over 30 years—clearly contributes to the CEO's success. Seven out of eight CEOs are still married to their first wives.

➤ While Episcopalians and Presbyterians are still over-represented among today's CEOs, their dominance is clearly less apparent than in earlier studies dating back to 1900.

➤ CEOs are considerably more religious than are average Americans. Furthermore, the more religious CEOs are better organized, more likely to be participative managers, and are even regarded as more humorous by their family and associates than are less religious CEOs. A spiritual dimension is clearly evident among most CEOs.

➤ The value of a college education is clearly illustrated by America's CEOs. Less than one in 100 CEOs failed to attend college. Business and engineering were the most popular majors. Many of today's CEOs have advanced degrees.

➤ Today's CEOs typically attended public schools and state colleges. Furthermore, most CEOs worked in high school and financed at least part of their college expenses.

➠ CEOs exhibited early signs of career success. They worked at an early age, participated in sports, and held offices in college clubs and other organizations.

➠ Most CEOs read and listen to music for pleasure, and exercise to stay in shape.

➠ CEOs are typically well organized, humorous, and creative. Some interesting relationships exist. For example, creativity and verbal ability are linked, as are being firstborn and having numerical ability.

➠ Finally, Theory Y (participative decision making) is the most common leadership pattern among CEOs.

While this profile is both interesting and insightful, the basic question remains: What does it all mean? While the authors did not intend to write a "how to succeed" book, certain bits of advice can be gleaned from looking at the successful careers of CEOs. Of course, it is important to realize that there are many paths to the top of any profession. But some items have clearly been associated with the executives who head the nation's business sector today, and to the extent that we can learn from their successes in order to better equip and prepare the next generation of aspiring executives, we've listed these items of advice as follows:

➠ To the extent that it is possible, a stable family background is desirable. While two-parent families were the norm for today's CEOs, it is obvious that future CEOs will reflect the family patterns that currently characterize U.S. society. It is probable that future CEOs will increasingly come from single parent and blended family backgrounds. The common denominator for success is a stable relationship with one's parents.

➠ Participation in team sports is particularly desirable. It is critical from not only a health perspective, but many CEOs stress that it teaches the value of teamwork and the role of competition.

➠ Participation in clubs and other activities is important. Again, extracurricular activities teach the value of teamwork.

➠ Both public and private elementary and secondary schools appear to do an adequate job of educating future business leaders.

➠ A college education is essential. Students with the appropriate aptitudes should be encouraged to pursue either business or engineering as an undergraduate. But increasingly, a bachelor's degree is not enough. An advanced degree is highly desirable. The choice of a specific college is less important than the type of degree selected.

➠ Young aspiring executives should be encouraged to work a few hours each week for pay at an early age. Later, they should be encouraged to earn at least some college expenses. It is clear from our study that future CEOs need to learn the importance of work early in their lives.

➠ A religious dimension is important; this element seems closely associated with the successful careers of today's CEOs.

Our study also suggested bits of wisdom for young managers climbing the corporate ladder.

➠ Get an advanced degree. Most metropolitan areas are serviced by evening MBA and law programs. A degree of this nature will give one a considerable advantage over others aspiring to the top positions in a corporation.

➠ Keep physically fit. Only one CEO in five exceeds reasonable weight standards for a person of his respective height. Exercise is also an excellent way to alleviate job-related stress.

➧ If married, future CEOs should spend considerable effort building relationships with their spouses. A stable marriage is one of the most significant factors linked to the successes of the CEOs in our study.

➧ Maintain or develop a religious dimension to one's life. Our research indicates that this factor is often linked with career success.

➧ Learn how to better organize work. With few exceptions, CEOs are well organized executives. They need to be in order to cope with the mounds of work that confront them. Numerous self-help books are available on the subject. Executives who currently lack good organizational habits are encouraged to consult such sources.

➧ Propose creative solutions to work problems. Creativity is a characteristic of America's CEOs, and the proposal of creative (but practical) solutions to work problems is an excellent way of obtaining recognition for future advancement.

➧ Practice Theory Y (participative) management. Most CEOs do. Managers aspiring to top corporate positions will find it desirable to acquire similar leadership traits.

APPENDIX

CEOS WHO COOPERATED IN THE BOOK

CEO	*COMPANY*
A	
Joseph F. Alibrandi	Whittaker
Wells P. Allen, Jr.	New York State Electric & Sons
Roy A. Anderson	Lockheed Corp.
Dwayne O. Andreas	Archer Daniels Midland Co.
William A. Andres	Dayton Hudson Corp.
Rand U. Araskog	International Telephone & Telegraph
Ronald G. Assaf	Sensormatic Electronics Corp.
Jesse I. Aweida	Storage Technology
B	
Louis F. Bantle	U.S. Tobacco Co.
Hugh A. Barker	Public Service Company of Indiana
Clarence C. Barksdale	Centerre Bank NA
Thomas J. Barlow	Anderson Clayton & Co.
John W. Bates, Jr.	Reading & Bates
Robert P. Bauman	AVCO Corp.
William B. Bechanan	Kentucky Utilities Co.
James R. Berrett	Computervision Corp.
James D. Berry	RepublicBank Corp.
Gene H. Bishop	TransOhio Financial Corp.
Warner B. Bishop	Mercantile Texas Corp.
William W. Boeschenstein	Owens-Corning Fiberglas
Lewis H. Bond	Texas American Bancshares, Inc.
William J. Bowen	Transco Energy Co.

CEO	COMPANY
John G. Breen	The Sherwin-Williams Co.
Bernard A. Bridgewater, Jr.	Brown Group, Inc.
Paul W. Briggs	Rochester Gas & Electric
W. L. Lyons Brown, Jr.	Brown-Forman Distillers Corp.
Wilson M. Brown, Jr.	Central National Bank
James E. Bruce	Idaho Power Co.
George A. Butler	First Pennsylvania Bank
C	
Thomas M. Cacioce	Allied Stores Corp.
Wilson K. Cadman	Kansas Gas and Electric Co.
Alexander W. Calder	Joy Manufacturing Co.
C. Clifford Cameron	First Union Corp.
Rafael Carrion, Jr.	Banco Popular de Puerto Rico
Albert V. Casey	American Airlines
John T. Cater	Southwest Bancshares, Inc.
Durwood Chalker	Central and South West Corp.
Robert A. Charpie	Cabot Corp.
Orson C. Clay	American National Insurance Co.
Robert B. Claytor	Norfolk Southern Corp.
Harry M. Conger	Homestake Mining Co.
William S. Cook	Union Pacific Corp.
Richard P. Cooley	Seattle-First National Bank
John A. Copeland	Swift Independent Packing Co.
Gordon L. Crenshaw	Universal Leaf Tobacco Co., Inc.
Gordon E. Crosby, Jr.	U S LIFE Corp.
Nevius M. Curtis	Delmarva Power & Light
Clifford A. Cutchins, III	Virginia National Bank
D	
Warner N. Dalhouse	Dominion Bankshares Corp.
Frederick Deane, Jr.	Bank of Virginia
William E. C. Dearden	Hershey Foods
Royce Diener	American Medical International
George H. Dixon	First Bank System, Inc.
Edward Donley	Air Products
James H. Duncan	First of America Bank Corp.
E	
Richard K. Eamer	National Medical Enterprises, Inc.
James A. Elkins, Jr.	First City Bancorporation of Texas, Inc.
John W. Ellis	Puget Sound Power & Light Co.
William B. Ellis	Northeast Utilities
John A. Elorriaga	U.W. Bancorp
Charles E. Exley, Jr.	NCR Corp.

CEO	COMPANY

F

Thomas F. Faught, Jr.	Dravo
Robert R. Ferguson, Jr.	First National State Bank of New Jersey
John H. Filer	Aetna Life & Casualty
Harold B. Finch, Jr.	Nash-Finch Co.
John E. Fisher	Nationwide
J. Robert Fluor	Fluor Corp.
T. Mitchell Ford	Emhart Corp.
Arthur Frankel	Pic'n'Save Corp.
Don C. Frisbee	Pacific Power & Light Co.
Thomas F. Frist, Jr.	Hospital Corporation of America
Thomas C. Frost	Cullen/Frost Bankers

G

Gale L. Galloway	Celeron Corp.
Robert W. Galvin	Motorola
James F. Gary	Pacific Resources, Inc.
Clarence J. Gauthier	NICOR
Jerry D. Geist	Public Service Company of New Mexico
Alexander F. Giacco	Hercules, Inc.
Merle E. Gilliand	Pittsburgh National Corp.
Robert M. Ginn	Cleveland Electric Illuminating Co.
Bram Goldsmith	City National Corp.
Henry C. Goodrich	Sonat Inc.
William R. Gould	Southern California Edison Co.
J. Peter Grace	W. R. Grace & Co.
Alex Grass	Rite Aid Corp.
Kenneth J. Griggy	Wilson Foods Corp.
N. Bud Grossman	Gelco Corp.

H

John R. Hall	Ashland Oil, Inc.
Richard D. Harrison	Fleming Companies, Inc.
Robert J. Harrison	Public Service of New Hampshire
Charles M. Harper	ConAgra, Inc.
N. Berne Hart	United Banks of Colorado
Fred L. Hartley	Union Oil Company of California
Raymond A. Hay	The LTV Corp.
Walter H. Helmerich, III	Helmerich & Payne, Inc.
Ralfph L. Hennebach	ASARCO, Inc.
Edward L. Hennessy, Jr.	Allied Chemical Corp.
Paul H. Henson	United Telecommunications, Inc.
Leonard G. Herring	Lowe's Companies, Inc.

CEO	COMPANY
Leo Hill	Affiliated Bankshares of Colorado
John J. Horan	Merck & Company, Inc.
Wesley J. Howe	Becton Dickinson and Co.
Harold J. Hudson, Jr.	General Reinsurance Co.
Robert D. Hunsucker	Panhandle Eastern Corp.
J	
George S. Jenks	Sunwest Financial Services, Inc.
Joseph A. Jennings	United Virginia Bankshares
K	
Charles J. Kane	Third National Bank
Herbert D. Kelleher	Southwest Airlines Co.
George M. Keller	Standard Oil of California
Ralph W. Ketner	Food Lion, Inc.
Peter D. Keirnan	Norstar Bancorp
William F. Kieschnick	Atlantic Richfield Co.
Abraham Krasnoff	Pall Corp.
L	
John P. Laborde	Tidewater, Inc.
M. Joseph Lapensky	Northwest Airlines, Inc.
Donald E. Lasater	Merchantile Trust Company, N.A.
Ronald C. Lassiter	Zapata Corp.
John P. LaWare	Shawmut Bank
William S. Lee	Duke Power
Henry F. LeMieux	Raymond International, Inc.
Donald D. Lennox	International Harvester
William E. Leonhard	Parsons
David S. Lewis	General Dynamics Corp.
Floyd W. Lewis	Middle South Utilities, Inc.
Sydnew Lewis	Best Products Company, Inc.
Lewis W. Lehr	Minnesota Mining & Manufacturing
Leonard Lieberman	Supermarkets General Corp.
William N. Liggett	First National Cincinnati
Richard G. Lindsley	Farmers Group, Inc.
Ben F. Love	Texas Commerce Bancshares, Inc.
Frank W. Luerssen	Inland Steel Co.
Peter A. Magoawn	Safeway Stores, Inc.
John P. Maloney	Deposit Guaranty National Bank
Robert H. Malott	FMC Corp. `
Frank J. Manaut	Bank of Hawaii
Alfred R. Manville	Fischbach Corp.
William A. Marguard	American Standard, Inc.
John P. Mascotte	The Continental Corp.
Daniel F. May	Republic Airlines

CEO   COMPANY

M

Warren E. McCain	Albertsons, Inc.
Julien L. McCall	National City Corp.
Donald W. McCarthy	Northern States Power Corp.
Walter J. McCarthy, Jr.	Detroit Edison
William C. McCord	Ensearch Corp.
John G. McCoy	Banc One
R. Gordon McGovern	Campbell Soup Co.
John A. McKinney	Manville Corp.
John W. McLean	Liberty National
William H. McMurren	Morrison-Knudsen Company, Inc.
Charles S. McNeer	Wisconsin Electric Power Co.
Paul D. Meek	American Petrofina, Inc.
Donald R. Melville	Norton Co.
Robert E. Mercer	The Goodyear Tire & Rubber Co.
Jerry D. Metcalf	S. M. Flickinger Company, Inc.
Morton H. Meyerson	Electronic Data Systems Corp.
Thomas M. Miller	Indiana National
David W. Mitchell	Avon Products, Inc.
James F. Montgomery	Great Western Financial Corp.
Gordon E. Moore	Intel Corp.
Jock Moseley	United States Fidelty and Guaranty Co.
Ray B. Mundt	Alco Standard Corp.
J. Terrence Murray	Fleet Financial

N

Edward Sheffield Nelson	Arkansas Louisiana Gas Co.
Joseph Neubauer	ARA Services
Guy W. Nichols	New England Electric
Roy Butler Noble	Affiliates, Inc.

O

Bernard J. O'Keefe	EG&G, Inc.
Dale R. Olseth	Medtronic, Inc.
John D. Ong	The B. F. Goodrich Co.
Paul F. Oreffice	The Dow Chemical Co.

P

C. Robert Palmer	Rowan Companies, Inc.
Sidney R. Petersen	Getty Oil Co.
Travis H. Petty	El Paso Natural Gas
William G. Phillips	International MultiFoods
T. Boone Pickens, Jr.	Mesa Petroleum
Lewis T. Preston	Morgan Guaranty Trust Co.

CEO	COMPANY
R	
Jack F. Reichert	Brunswick Corp.
Robert P. Reuss	Centel Corp.
Victor J. Riley, Jr.	Key Banks, N.A.
Burnell R. Roberts	Mead Corp.
David M. Roderick	USX Corp.
Ian M. Rolland	Lincoln National Corp.
Francis C. Rooney, Jr.	Melville Corp.
John E. Rupert	Broadview Savings and Loan Co.
Robert D. Rowan	Fruehauf Corp.
Jack F. Rowe	Minnesota Power
S	
Frank P. Samford, Jr.	Torchmark Corp.
Wendell J. Satre	The Washington Water Power Co.
Henry B. Schacht	Cummins Engine Company, Inc.
Robert M. Schaeberle	Nabisco Brands, Inc.
Herbert H. Schiff	SCOA Industries, Inc.
Edmund A. Schroer	Northern Indiana Public Service Co.
Philip F. Searle	Flagship Banks, Inc.
Arthur R. Seder, Jr.	American Natural Resources
Sam F. Segnar	InterNorth
Donald V. Seibert	J.C. Penney
John D. Selby	Consumers Power Co.
George J. Sella	American Cyanamid Co.
T. Joseph Semrod	United Jersey Banks
Teruhisa Shimizu	Sumitomo Bank California
Robert H. Short	Portland General Electric Co.
Forrest N. Shumway	The Signal Companies, Inc.
Edwin H. Shutt	Tampax, Inc.
Thomas C. Simons	Capital Holding Corp.
Roy W. Simmons	Zions Utah Bancorp
George R. Slater	The Marine Corp.
John G. Sloneker	Ohio Casualty Corp.
S. Bruce Smark, Jr.	Continental Group
Richard A. Smith	General Cinema Corp.
Charles E. Sporck	National Semiconductor
David Stanley	Payless Cashways, Inc.
Dearn R. Stichnoth	Iowa-Illinois Gas & Electric Co.
Robert P. Straetz	Textron, Inc.
Robert Strickland	Trust Company of Georgia
Arthur O. Sulzberger	The New York Times

CEO	*COMPANY*
T	
W. Reid Thompson	Potomac Electric Power Co.
Zane G. Todd	Indianapolis Power & Light Co.
Eugene A. Tracy	The Peoples Gas Light and Coke Co.
Roland M. Trafton	Safeco Insurance Co.
G. Robert Truex, Jr.	Rainier Bancorp
Stewart Turley	Jack Eckerd Corp.
Jack Twyman	Super Food Services, Inc.
V	
Alfred W. Van Sinderen	Southern New England Telephone
W	
Richard F. Walker	Public Service Company of Colorado
Evern R. Wall	El Paso Electric Co.
William E. Wall	Kansas Power & Light
John C. Wallace	Petrolane, Inc.
M. Brock Weir	AmeriTrust of Cleveland
Gordon E. Wells	CharterCorp
Dr. W. Clarke Wescoe	Sterling Drug, Inc.
L. Stanton Williams	PPG Industries, Inc.
Thomas R. Williams	The First National Bank of Atlanta
John P. Williamson	Toledo Edison
Thornton A. Wilson	The Boeing Co.
Frank Wobst	Huntington Bancshares
John F. Woodhouse	Sysco
Michael J. Wright	Super Valu Stores, Inc.
Myron A. Wright	Cameron Iron Works, Inc.
Y	
Herbert J. Young	Gibralter Financial Corp. of California
Z	
Erwin Zaban	National Services Industries, Inc.
Raymond Zimmerman	Service Merchandise Company, Inc.

BIBLIOGRAPHY

Chapter 1

Branco, Anthony. "Jerry Tsai: The Comeback Kid." *Business Week*, 18 August 1986, 72–78.

"Birth Order and Intelligence." *Science News*, 27 March 1982, 218.

Burck, Charles G. "A Group Profile of the Fortune 500 Chief Executives." *Fortune*, May 1986, 173–77, 308–12.

Byrne, John A. "Fathers and Sons." *Forbes*, 28 January 1985, 94–95.

Davis, Flora. "The Personality Power of Birth Order." *Madamoiselle*, February 1983, 115–17, 198.

Fisher, Maria. "The Mother Lode." *Forbes*, 20 May 1985, 229.

Fleenor, C. Patrick, David L. Kurtz, and Louis E. Boone. "The Changing Profile of Business Leadership." *Business Horizons*, July-August 1983, 43–46.

Hall, Elizabeth. "Mining New Gold from Old Research." *Psychology Today*, February 1986, 46–51.

Hall, Trish. "As Middle Children Become Rarer, Society May Miss Their Influence." *The Wall Street Journal*, 21 August 1986, 25.

Harris, Irving. *The Promised Seed*. London: The Free Press, 1964.

Harris, Marilyn A., and Christopher Power. "He Hated Losing—Even in Touch Football." *Business Week*, 30 June 1986.

Harris, Marilyn A., et al. "Can Jack Welch Reinvent GE?" *Business Week*, 30 June 1986, 62–67.

Henry, Sherrye. "How They Began." *Parade Magazine*, 1 February 1987, 4–6.

Historical Statistics of the United States: Colonial Times to 1970, Part I, 41.

U.S. Bureau of the Census. *Household and Family Characteristics* P-20, no. 388 (March 1983): 132, table 12.

Kurtz, David L., and Louis E. Boone. "A Profile of Business Leadership." *Business Horizons*, September/October 1981, 28–32.

Lackenberger, Margaret E. "An Analysis of Self-Actualizing Dimensions of Top and Middle Management Personnel." Ph.D. diss., North Texas State Universtiy, 1970.

Leman, Kevin. *The Birth Order Book*. New York: Dell Publishing Co., Inc., 1985.

Leonard, Burr, Rita Koselka, and Edward Cone. "The Top 25." *Forbes*, 15 June 1987, 150–58.

Machan, Dyan. "Educate, Preach and Pray." *Forbes*, 9 March 1987, 146, 148.

McComas, Maggie. "Atop the Fortune 500: A Survey of the CEOs." *Fortune*, 28 April 1986, 26–31.

"Middle Children's Middling Self-Esteem." *Psychology Today*, September 1982, 16.

Nibley, MaryBeth. "Midwest is Breeding Ground of U.S. Executives, Survey Says." *Journal-American*, 29 January 1987, C3

Ryan, Joan. "Firstborn or Last: Place in Family Affects Character." *The Seattle Times*, 24 May 1985, E1.

"Smarter Kids from Small Families, Study Says." *Journal-American*, 28 May 1985, A1-A2.

Sutton-Smith, Brian, and B. G. Rosenberg. *The Sibling*. New York: Holt, Rinehart and Winston, 1970.

"The Forbes Four Hundred." *Forbes*, 1 October 1984, 76–162.

Chapter 2

Burck, Charles G. "A Group Profile of the Fortune 500 Chief Executives." *Fortune*, May 1976, 173–77, 308–12.

Coleman, Richard P., and Bernice Neugarten. *Social Status in the City*. San Francisco: Jossey-Bass, 1971.

Coleman, Richard P., and Lee Rainwater. *Standing in America's New Dimensions of Class*. New York: Basic Books, 1978.

"The Forbes Four Hundred." *Forbes*, 1 October 1984, 76–162.

Henry, Sherrye. "How They Began." *Parade Magazine*, 1 February 1987, 4–6.

Krohe, James, Jr. "Take My Boss—Please." *Across The Board*, February 1987, 31–35.

Leonard, Burr, Rita Koskelka, and Edward Cone. "The Top 25." *Forbes*, 15 June 1987, 150–58.

McComas, Maggie. "Atop the Fortune 500: A Survey of the CEOs." *Fortune*, 28 April 1986, 26–31.

Newcomer, Mabel. *The Big Business Executive.* New York: Columbia University Press, 1955.

"Who Owns Corporate America." *U.S. News & World Report,* 21 July 1986, 36–38.

Chapter 3

Baker, Steve. "Sick Jokes Can Be Healthy at Times." *Mobile Press-Register,* 18 May 1986, G1.

Bernstein, C. "Power Romance." *People,* 2 February 1987, 100–102.

"Fascinating Figures, FYI." *Reader's Digest,* July 1985, 39. Condensed from *Harper's Index, Harper's Magazine.*

Fincher, Jack. *Lefties: The Origins and Consequences of Being Left-Handed.* New York: G. P. Putnam's Sons, 1977, 26–27.

"The Forbes Four Hundred." *Forbes,* 1 October 1984, 76–162.

Herron, Jeannine, ed. *Neuropsychology of Left Handedness.* New York: Academic Press, 1980.

Higgins, Kevin T. "Southpaws Left Out By Marketers." *Marketing News,* 30 August 1985, 6.

"How Fat Cats Stay Thin." *Business Week,* 28 October 1985, 124–25.

Johnson, Sheila. "Hey Boss, Did You See This Story About—Oops, Uh, Nothing, Boss." *The Wall Street Journal,* 11 July 1985, 29.

Kurtz, David L. "Physical Appearance and Stature: Important Variables in Sales Recruiting." *Personnel Journal,* December 1969, 981–84.

Lerbinger, Otto, and Nathaniel H. Sperber. *Key to the Executive Head.* Readway, Mass.: Addison-Wesley Publishing, 1975.

"Life Among the Business Elite." *The Wall Street Journal,* 20 March 1987, 20D.

McCarthy, Michael J. "A CEO's Life: Money, Security and Meetings." *The Wall Street Journal,* 7 July 1987, 31.

McComas, Maggie. "Atop the Fortune 500: A Survey of the CEOs." *Fortune,* 28 April 1986, 26-31.

Rychlak, Joseph F. *Personality and Lifestyle of Young Male Managers.* New York: Academic Press, Inc., 1982.

Bureau of Labor Statistics. *Statistical Abstract of the United States: 1984,* 128, 200.

Sheridan, Mike. "James R. Moffett, Chairman and CEO, Freeport-McMoRan, Inc." *Sky,* July 1986, 40.

Steckel, Richard H. "Height and Per Capita Income." National Bureau of Economic Research. *Reprint No. 354.* Reprinted from *Historical Methods,* Winter 1983, 1–7.

"This Is No Tall Story: A New Book Claims Your Height Can Affect Your Job, Salary, and Life." *People,* 28 April 1980, 83–87.

Vander Zanden, James W. *Human Development.* New York: Alfred A. Knopf, Inc., 1985, 165.

Chapter 4

"Bedtime for the Boss." *The Conference Board,* April 1987, 8.

Beeman, Don R. "Is the Social Drinker Killing Your Company?" *Business Horizons,* January-February 1985, 54–58.

"Business Bulletin." *The Wall Street Journal,* 24 December 1981, 1.

Covey, Lirio S., and Ernest L. Wynder. "Smoking Habits and Occupational Status." *Journal of Occupational Medicine,* August 1981, 537–42.

Downey, Charles. "All Worked-Up Over Work." *American Way,* 15 February 1985, 85–89.

"Few Top Managers Are Smokers." *American Medical News,* 16 May 1986, 11.

Freedman, Alix M. "Harmful Habit: Cigarette Smoking Is Growing Hazardous to Careers in Business." *The Wall Street Journal,* 23 April 1987, 1, 19.

Hall, Trish. "Smoking of Cigarettes Seems to be Becoming a Lower-Class Habit." *The Wall Street Journal,* 25 June 1985, 1, 16.

Hildebrandt, Herbert W., et al. *The Newly Promoted Executive: A Study in Corporate Leadership, 1985–1986.* Ann Arbor: The University of Michigan, 0000.

Hutchins, Dexter. "The Drive to Kick Smoking at Work." *Fortune,* 15 September 1986, 43–53.

Kiechel, Walter III. "Looking Out for the Executive Alcoholic." *Fortune,* 11 January 1982, 117–20.

Kleinfeld, Sonny. *Staying at the Top: The Life of a CEO.* New York: The New American Library, 1986, 155–57.

"Life Among the Business Elite." *The Wall Street Journal,* 20 March 1987, 20D.

Statistical Abstract of the United States: 1984, 127, table 198. Bureau of Labor Statistics, U.S. Government.

"Survey Shows CEOs Fit as Fiddles and Avoid Cigarettes." *Industry Week,* 23 August 1982, 26–27.

Weis, William L. "Can You Afford to Hire Smokers?" *Personnel Administrator,* May 1981, 71–78.

———. "Smoking: Burning a Hole in the Balance Sheet." *Personnel Management,* May 1981, 24–29.

Weis, William L., and C. Patrick Fleenor. "Cold Shouldering the Smoker." *Supervisory Management,* September 1981, 31–35.

Chapter 5

Bartolome, Fernando. "The Work Alibi: When It's Harder to Go Home." *Harvard Business Review,* March-April 1983, 67–74.

Bennis, Warren. "Good Managers and Good Leaders." *Across the Board,* October 1984, 7–11.

"The Biggest Bosses." *Fortune,* 3 August 1987.

"The Corporate Boss—What Makes Him Tick." *U.S. News & World Report,* 30 April 1984, 18.

Downey, Charles. "All Worked Up Over Work." *American Way,* 5 February 1985, 85–89.

"The Forbes Four Hundred." *Forbes,* 1 October 1984, 76–162.

Heatherly, Mike. "John Ellis: He Holds the Power at Puget." *Journal-American,* 2 February 1986.

Hildebrandt, Herbert W., et al. *The Newly Promoted Executive: A Study in Corporate Leadership.* Ann Arbor: The University of Michigan, 1986.

Ingrossia, Laurence. "Aftermath of Failure: The Collapse of a Man, The Agony of a Family." *The Wall Street Journal,* 12 March 1982, 1, 14.

Ladenberger, Margaret E. "An Analysis of Self-Actualizing Dimensions of Top and Middle Management Personnel." Ph.D. diss., North Texas State University, 1970.

Lublin, Joann S. "Labor Letter." *The Wall Street Journal,* 3 August 1982, 1.

"The Man Behind the Takeover." *The Seattle Times,* 26 February 1986, B3.

National Center for Health Statistics, Monthly Vital Statistics Report. *Advance Report of Final Divorce Statistics: 1981.*

McCarthy, Michael J. "A CEO's Life: Money, Security and Meetings." *The Wall Street Journal,* 7 July 1987, 31.

O'Reilly, Brian. "A Body Builder Lifts Greyhound." *Fortune,* 28 October 1985. Rychlak, Joseph F. *Personality and Lifestyle of Young Male Managers.* New York: Academic Press, Inc., 1982.

Schmid, Randolph. "Survey Finds Marriage Delayed, More Kids with One Parent." *Journal-American,* 10 December 1986, A1.

Sheridan, Mike. "James R. Moffett, Chairman and CEO, Freeport-McMoRan, Inc." *SKY,* July 1986, 40, 42, 46.

Worthy, Ford S. "You're Probably Working Too Hard." *Fortune,* 27 April 1987, 133–140.

Chapter 6

Baig, Edward C. "Profiting with Help from Above." *Fortune,* 27 April 1987, 36–46.

Barrett, David, ed. *World Christian Encyclopedia.* New York: Oxford University Press, 1982, 711.

Burck, Charles G. "A Group Profile of the Fortune 500 Chief Executives." *Fortune*, May 1976, 173-77, 308-12.

"The Corporate Boss—What Makes Him Tick." *U.S. News & World Report*, April 1984, 18.

"The Forbes Four Hundred." *Forbes*, 1 October 1984, 76–162.

Getschow, George. "Cardinals' Friend: J. Peter Grace Shows How Big Names Raise Big Money for Charity." *The Wall Street Journal*, 8 May 1987, 1, 14.

Ingrassia, Laurence. "Executive's Crisis: Aftermath of a Failure: The Collapse of a Man, The Agony of a Family." *The Wall Street Journal*, 12 March 1982, 14.

Kallen, Barbara. "Praying for Guidance." *Forbes*, 1 December 1986, 220–21.

Lerbinger, Otto, and Nathaniel H. Sperber. *Key to the Executive Head.* Reading, Mass.: Addison-Wesley Publishing Co., 1975.

"Life Among the Business Elite." *The Wall Street Journal*, 20 March 1987, 20D.

Newcomer, Mabel. *The Big Business Executive.* New York: Columbia University Press, 1955.

Petre, Peter. "America's Most Successful Entrepreneur." *Fortune*, 27 October 1986, 26–27.

Rychlak, Joseph F. *Personality and Lifestyle of Young Male Managers.* New York: Academic Press, Inc., 1982.

Statistical Abstract of the United States: 1984, 58, table 80.

Statistical Abstract of the United States: 1986, 51, table 77.

Sutton-Smith, Brian, and B. G. Rosenberg. *The Sibling.* New York: Holt, Rinehart and Winston, Inc., 1970, 78.

Chapter 7

Burck, Charles G. "A Group Profile of the Fortune 500 Chief Executives." *Fortune*, May 1976 173-77, 308-12.

Byrne, John A. "Let's Hear It for Liberal Arts." *Forbes*, 1 July 1985, 112, 114.
_____. "Fathers and Sons." *Forbes*, 28 January 1985, 94–95.

"The Corporate Boss—What Makes Him Tick." *U.S. News & World Report*, 30 April 1984, 18.

Dennis, Darienne L. "The Man Who Brought GE to Life." *Fortune*, 5 January 1987, 76, 78.

U.S. Department of Commerce, Bureau of the Census. *Educational Attainment in the United States*, P-29, no. 390 (March 1980): 18; (March 1981): 12.

Enrico, Roger. "Follow Me! The Path of a Leader." *Across the Board*, January 1987, 22–28.

"The Forbes Four Hundred." *Forbes*, 1 October 1984, 76–162.

"Harvard, Yale Lead Colleges Producing Executives." *The Chronicle of Higher Education*, 16 October 1985, 2.

Heidrick and Struggles, Inc. *Mobile Manager*, 1985, 4.

Kiechell, Walter III. "Executives Without Degrees." *Fortune*, 28 June 1982, 119–20.

"The Latest Worry for Parents of Teens." *Fortune*, 2 February 1987, 10.

Leonard, Burr, Rita Koselka, and Edward Cone. "The Top 25." *Forbes*, 15 June 1987, 150–58.

Lerbinger, Otto, and Nathaniel H. Sperber. *Key to the Executive Head*. Reading, Mass.: Addison-Wesley Publishing Co., 1975.

"Life Among the Business Elite." *The Wall Street Journal*, 20 March 1974, 20D.

"Most Top Executives Learned to Play Ball in High School." *USA Today*, 21 July 1987, 7B.

Newcomer, Mabel. *The Big Business Executive*. New York: Columbia University Press, 1955, 69.

"Profile of CEOs." *The Wall Street Journal*, 28 October 1985, 23.

U.S. Department of Commerce, Bureau of Labor Statistics. *Statistical Abstract of the United States: 1984*.

Weschler, Pat. "The Long Haul to the Top." *Dun's Business Month*, April 1984, 52–71.

Chapter 8

Byrne, John A. "Executive Sweat." *Forbes*, 15 May 1985, 198–200.
_____. "It Ain't Over Until It's Over." *Forbes*, 15 July 1985, 101–4.

"The Forbes Four Hundred." *Forbes*, 1 October 1984, 76–162.

"Most Top Executives Learned to Play Ball in High School." *USA Today*, 21 July 1987, 7B.

National Center for Educational Statistics. *Two Years After High School: A Capsule Description of 1980 Seniors*. Division of Educational Statistics, U.S. Office of Education.

Sheridan, Mike. "James R. Moffett: Chairman & CEO, Freeport-McMoRan, Inc." *SKY*, July 1986, 40–46.

"Tony Burns Has Ryder's Rivals Eating Dust." *Business Week*, 6 April 1987, 104.

Zemper, Eric. Information provided by Zemper, the NCAA's Research Coordinator.

Chapter 9

"The Art of Managing." *Across the Board*, July/August 1985, 35–42.

Balwin, William. "The Greener Pastures Syndrome." *Forbes*, 5 May 1986, 91–93.

"The Biggest Bosses." *Fortune*, 3 August 1987.

Bock, Gordon. "A Brash and Brainy 'Brat'" *Time*, 1 June 1987, 50.

"Book Buyers." *The Wall Street Journal*, 1 October 1985, 33.

Brophy, Beth. "Workaholics Beware: Long Hours May Not Pay." *U.S. News & World Report*, 7 April 1986, D1, D8.

Byrne, John A. "Executive Sweat." *Forbes*, 20 May 1985, 198–200.

Downey, Charles. "All Worked Up Over Work." *American Way*, 5 February 1985, 85–89.

Ehrlich, Arnold. "Workaholism—A Rampant Malady." *Forbes*, 20 July 1981, 20.

Getschow, George. "Cardinals' Friend: J. Peter Grace Shows How Big Names Raise Big Money for Charity." *The Wall Street Journal*, 8 May 1987, 1, 14.

Greene, Richard. "Does Physically Fit Mean Fiscally Fit?" *Forbes*, 22 September 1986, 189.

Heidrick and Struggles, Inc. *CEO: Findings of a Survey of the Chief Executive Officers of America's Largest Industrial and Service Organizations*, 1984.

Hillkirk, John. "Akio Morita." *USA Today*, 29 October 1986, 4B.

Kurtz, David L., Louis E. Boone, and C. Patrick Fleenor. "The Complete Manager's Bookshelf." *Business Horizons*, May/June 1983, 33–35.

"Labor Letter." *The Wall Street Journal*, 5 August 1986, 1.

Lerbinger, Otto, and Nathaniel H. Sperber. *Key to the Executive Head*. Reading, Mass.: Addison-Wesley Publishing Co., 1975, 123–53.

"Life Among the Business Elite." *The Wall Street Journal*, 20 March 1987, 20D.

McCarthy, Michael J. "A CEO's Life: Money, Security and Meetings." *The Wall Street Journal*, 7 August 1987, 31.

McDermott, Terry. "Shrontz: Taking Over at Boeing." *The Seattle Times/Seattle Post Intelligencer*, 2 March 1986, D1, D8.

McManus, Kevin. "What Makes CEOs Run?" *Forbes*, 29 March 1982, 126–32.

Mosak, Brian S. "Least Successful Execs Show High Zest for Life." *Industry Week*, 20 February 1984, 27.

Nader, Ralph, and William Taylor. *The Big Boys*. New York: Pantheon Books, 1986, 155.

Perham, John. "Executive Health Audit." *Dun's Business Month*, October 1984, 88–112.

Pratt, Edmund T., Jr., interviewed by David Finn. *Across the Board*, December 1985, 37.

Sherman, Beth. "What Vacationing Executives are Reading." *The New York Times*, 14 July 1985, sec. 3, 13.

Solomon, Julie. "Working at Relaxation." *The Wall Street Journal Report on Business*, 21 April 1986, 1–2.

"Survey Shows CEOs Fit as Fiddles and Avoid Cigarettes." *Industry Week*, 23 August 1982, 26–27.

Toufexis, Anastasia. "The Shape of the Nation." *Time*, 7 October 1985, 60–61.

Toy, Steward, James R. Norma, and Terri Thompson. "Armand Hammer at 87: Still Showing Them How to Do Deals." *Business Week*, 20 January 1986, 68–71.

Warner, Rawleigh Jr., interviewed by David Finn. *Across the Board*, November 1985, 47.

Wellemeyer, Marilyn. "Books Bosees Read." *Fortune*, 27 April 1987, 145–48.

Willis, Chris. "Inside the Troubled Empire of Peter Grace." *Business Week*, 16 June 1986, 68–71.

Chapter 10

"The Biggest Bosses." *Fortune*, 3 August 1987.

Burck, Charles G. "A Group Profile of the Fortune 500 Chief Executives." *Fortune*, May 1976, 173-77, 308-12.

Downey, Charles. "All Worked Up Over Work." *American Way*, 15 February 1985, 85–89.

Enrico, Roger. "Follow Me! The Path of a Leader." *Across the Board*, January 1987, 22–28.

"The Forbes Four Hundred." *Forbes*, 1 October 1984, 76–162.

Horowitz, Bruce. "Why Some CEOs Fail." *Industry Week*, 31 October 1983, 53–57.

Kirton, M. J., and Glenn Mulligan. "Correlates of Managers Attitudes Toward Change." *Journal of Applied Psychology* 58, no. 1 (1973): 101–7.

Lamb, Robert Boyden. "CEOs for This Season." *Across the Board*, April 1987, 34–41.

Leonard, Burr, Rita Koselka, and Edward Cone. "The Top 25." *Forbes*, 15 June 1987, 150–58.

Lerbinger, Otto, and Nathaniel H. Sperber. *Key to the Executive Head*. Reading, Mass.: Addison-Wesley Publishing Co., 1975.

McCarthy, Michael J. "A CEO's Life: Money, Security and Meetings." *The Wall Street Journal*, 7 July 1987, 31.

McDermott, Terry. "The Cream of the Corporate Crop." *Pacific*, 10 August 1986, 4–9.

Morrison, Ann M. "CEOs Pick the Best CEOs." *Fortune*, 4 May 1981, 133–36.

"Who Holds the Power Outside Washington." *U.S. News & World Report*, 20 May 1985, 58–61.

Epilogue

Baum, Laurie. "Corporate Women: They're About to Break Through to the Top." *Business Week*, 22 June 1987, 72–88.

Bennett, Amanda. "Losing Ground? Surveyed Firms Report Fewer Women Directors." *The Wall Street Journal*, 17 July 1987, 23.

"The Biggest Bosses." *Fortune*, 3 August 1987.

Brophy, Beth, with Nancy Linnon. "Why Women Execs Stop Before the Top." *U.S. News & World Report*, 29 December 1986, 72–73.

Machan, Dyan. "Peripatetic Banker." *Forbes*, 1 June 1987, 170, 197.

Schwartz, Felice N. "Don't Write Off Women as Leaders." *Fortune*, 8 June 1987, 185, 188.

Sellers, Patricia. "The Rag Trade's Reluctant Revolutionary." *Fortune*, 5 January 1987, 36–38.